An Intelligent Person's Guide
to Liberalism

An Intelligent Person's Guide to Liberalism

Conrad Russell

Duckworth

First published in 1999 by
Gerald Duckworth & Co. Ltd.
61 Frith Street, London W1V 5TA
Tel: 0171 434 4242
Fax: 0171 434 4420
Email: enquiries@duckworth-publishers.co.uk

A catalogue record for this book is available
from the British Library

ISBN 0 7156 2947 6

Typeset by Ray Davies
Printed in Great Britain by
Biddles Limited, Guildford & King's Lynn

Contents

To Bob Maclennan
'Some are born Liberal'

Preface

The Minister who serves opposite me in the Lords is also a fellow-academic. When I take her to task for what she has not done, she compares me to a reviewer scolding her for not writing the book she did not attempt to write. When this book appears, I may understand how she feels.

This is not a work of academic history. The ground it covers is outside my area of professional expertise, and any authority I may have in it is that of a politician rather than of a historian. More seriously, the motive for this book has not been the pure academic one of understanding what happened, but rather one of trying to identify a continuous tradition. That is an ahistorical motive, and it pollutes the well of pure academic history. I have of course tried to make my statements true, and for any verifiable point of fact, I have tried to rely on competent academic authority. I have found a burgeoning of high quality research on which to draw. Nevertheless, the perspective which makes academic history is not here, and I must not pretend otherwise.

Nor is this a work of current politics. Anyone who wants to know current Liberal Democrat policy will do better with the flood of policy papers out of Cowley Street than with this book. It is rather an attempt to answer the question cantankerously asked by George Bernard Shaw in 1906: 'What are the Liberals *for*?' What is the creed for which it stands, the essence by which one Liberal may recognise another across the centuries? That such an essence does in fact exist is something of which writing this book has made me more certain than I ever was before. The sense of recognition has often been overwhelming. How far one man's vision is the same thing as the essence of Liberalism is not a question for me to answer. That is a question for my readers. I hope to learn from them.

I have incurred debts to many people. Perhaps my greatest is to Bob Maclennan, who has for some time been encouraging me to write such a book as this. In gratitude, I have asked him to accept the dedication. I await his judgement with some anxiety. He is a very good judge of what is good Liberalism. I would like to thank Robin Baird-Smith, who created the opportunity to write this book. I hope the result will repay his confidence.

I have incurred many debts in the course of pursuing this subject. I would like to thank my academic colleagues Arthur Burns, Miles Taylor and Peter Clarke for advice, information, bibliography and encouragement. For the failings, I alone am responsible.

Party philosophy, like the sense of a Quaker Meeting, evolves out of long discussion and good friendship. I would like to thank my hosts at innumerable party functions for reactions which have been constructive, informative and helpful. I would like to thank Duncan Brack, formerly Director of Policy and Secretary of the Liberal Democrat History Group, for encouraging me, ten years ago, to feed my knowledge of history into the task of expressing party philosophy. He has started something which is still going on. My debts to friends and colleagues are more numerous than I can mention, but I owe special thanks to the late Nancy Seear, who taught me my craft. I have also learnt from Alan Beith, Edward Davey, Helen Bailey, Eric Avebury, Shirley Williams, Anthony Lester, Kiron Reid, Alex Wilcock, Jackie Ballard and Ruth Coleman, and from many others. The list grows daily, and I would like to thank them all.

July 1999   Conrad Russell

Introduction

'Liberalism', like 'democracy', is a hurrah-word. The intention to signify that the thing described is good is always clearer than the identity of the thing described. The things praised as 'liberalism' differ as much as the people's democracies of eastern Europe differed from the representative democracy of the United Kingdom. If there is anything in common between the 'liberalism' of Milton Friedman and that of J.K. Galbraith, it is not apparent to me.

Even descent from the heroes of the liberal pantheon is not necessarily sufficient. The 'liberalism' of Lord Harris of High Cross and his free market economics and the moral 'liberalism' of Roy Jenkins' Home Secretaryship both stake claims to the mantle of John Stuart Mill, yet again, if there is any common ground between them, it is not perceptible to me, or, I believe, to them.

The lexicographer's approach to identifying liberalism, which would analyse all the meanings given to the word 'liberalism' and seek for a lowest common denominator, is therefore doomed to failure. A clever advocate might attempt the task, but the common ground he would impose would, in the end, be a sanctification of his own prejudices. It would be an application of what Jeremy Bentham called 'the principle of sympathy and antipathy'. An attempt to seek out the 'true' meaning of liberalism would be subject to the same reproach: it would codify what the writer thought 'ought' to be the true meaning of the word. Such imposition of one's own prejudices is an illiberal proceeding. We all do it, but we should not do it any more than we can help.

We need a touchstone and, though all touchstones are arbitrary, some are less arbitrary than others. We need the least arbitrary we can find. The one chosen here is the ideas which have given continuity to the Liberal Party in its various forms since 1679. This allows the founders of the party and their successors the privilege given to Adam in the *Book of Genesis*, of naming the creatures over whom they found themselves presiding. This will at least provide a touchstone with a certain second-order objectivity. Even those who think it fails the primary test of defining the essence of 'liberalism' may recognise that it passes the second-order and by no means useless test of defining the essence of a major political party. Even if this may not be the same as a platonic essence of liberalism (assuming that is not a contradiction in terms), one may hope that the two have a resemblance which is more than purely coincidental.

This is not to claim that there has ever been a time when all liberals were in the Liberal Party. Whatever definition we take, that has manifestly never been the case, and is certainly not the case today. What the claim does say is that if we identify such people as 'liberals', we do so in virtue of qualities or opinions which have some point of overlap with the defining marks of the Liberal Party. This at least is a question which goes far enough beyond my personal prejudices to be susceptible of genuine intellectual enquiry.

Within the Liberal International, the major criticism will be that this identifies British, rather than international, liberalism. This criticism is of course valid, and the reader should bear it in mind throughout. The anti-clerical republicanism of, for example, Mazzini represented a liberalism very different from that of Russell or Palmerston, and within the Liberal International, these and many other liberalisms are blended together into a whole.

I have two defences to offer to this charge, neither totally adequate but I hope both worth a hearing. First, there is a resemblance between the different members of this family, as both Mazzini and Russell recognised. Since the British version came first, it has inevitably made a large contribution to the task of defining the touchstone by which others have decided whether they wanted admission to the liberal family. Second, there is sense in writers writing of what we know. The task of searching for the essence of British Liberalism as it has developed over the past 320 years is big enough for my knowledge, for my time, or for the space which I have been allotted. That is all I will try to do.

1

The Empty Hearse

With six months to go, I think it may now be said that Liberalism, as an organised political force operating through its own political party, has survived the twentieth century. It has been a white-knuckle ride.

I first heard of the existence of the Liberal Party when I was eight. My parents were sitting over the paper looking at the results of the 1945 election. They were mourning Liberal defeats, and especially that of Sir Archibald Sinclair, then leader of the party, whom they described as 'a good man'. They said the party was finished.

I supposed, eight-year-olds do, that the grown-ups knew what they were talking about. I remember also the moment, I think in 1951, when I first began to wonder whether they were right. Nancy Seear, who 37 years later was to become my Deputy Leader in the House of Lords and who taught me my political craft, had fought a seat in the London area and polled over 10,000 votes. The *Evening Standard* had grossly misspelt her name. My first thought was: 'That's an unusual name – I wonder how it's really spelt?' My next was that perhaps the party was not finished after all, and I ought to learn some more about it. It proved, on the information available in the 1950s, surprisingly difficult. It was possible to find out party policy on individual issues by *very* careful reading of the papers, but the party's basic values and principles were very hard to discover. Publishers did not then generally think there was a market for such things, and if they do now, that is a sign of how much things have changed. It was also difficult for the party to explain its basic values because the questions asked of it were resolutely set in a two-party right-left class-based polarity, into which the party adamantly refused to fit. This meant that all questions about basic values were oblique to what Liberals really wanted to say. It is the first purpose of this book to make life easier for anyone coming fresh to the subject, and wanting to ask the questions I was asking as a thirteen-year-old in 1951.

It is after 1951 that the party's obstinate refusal to go away is most remarkable. Every Liberal remembers Aneurin Bevan's jibe about getting to the House in one taxi, and Jeremy Thorpe's remark that 'every year the hearse turns up at the Liberal Assembly, and every year it goes away empty'. If the test of the true church is persecution, the test of the true party is adversity. Those who never wavered all through the dark days from 1951 to 1974 (of whom I cannot claim to be one, but from whom I have learnt a vast amount) were sustained by the two convictions, that they spoke for one of the world's major political philosophies, and that no other party would ever adequately express that philosophy. The principles which brought a party through this must have very considerable power.

This sense of a party hanging on by its fingertips for the sake of the principles it is defending goes back to the General Election of 1918. Those who seek deep underlying reasons for the difficulties of Liberalism in the twentieth century do not always remember how much, in the General Election of 1918, to borrow Roy Jenkins' phrase, 'we shot ourselves, not in the foot, but somewhere very near the heart'. Our troubles in 1918 arose from the fact that in the wartime coalition, Lloyd George had become Prime Minister while Asquith remained party leader. On the conclusion of the war, Lloyd George decided to carry on the wartime coalition with the Conservatives while omitting to get the assent of the party to this course. As a result, we fought the General Election of 1918 as two rival parties, competing for votes against each other, one led by the party leader, and the other by the Prime Minister. We went into that election with a majority. We came out of it with the two parties between them polling less than we did in the Local Elections of 1999. This, too, is something it is remarkable that any party could survive.

Here again, it was the commitment to Liberal principle which kept the party afloat. Violet Markham, writing to Elizabeth Haldane in 1922, captured this feeling exactly: 'I cling, like yourself, to the party, for great though its weakness at the moment, and deplorable though the lack of vision in our unsatisfactory leaders, liberalism as a *faith* and a *principle* is that I cannot give up.'[1]

The wilderness years from 1918 to 1974 were the years of class politics, and for many Liberals, it was the basing of politics on class which they could not accept. Asquith in 1921 said: 'The Liberal Party is not today, it never has been, and so long as I have any connection with it, it never will be the party of any class, rich or poor, great or small, numerous or sparse in its composition. We are a party of no class.'[2] This was both gut reaction and party tradition. A party which, from its very beginning in pressing for equal civil rights for Nonconformists, had been a party of non-discrimination simply could not accommodate an approach which judged people simply as members of a category, regardless of anything they did, said, thought or achieved. It risked infringing what Professor Biagini has called 'the old Whig cry of "equality before the law" '.[3]

It also infringed the instinctive Liberal assumption that people associated together in politics on the basis, not of birth, but of belief. Again in Professor Biagini's words, 'what held the rank and file together were the values shared by activists, electors and supporters in general, rather than the material interests of the groups to which they belonged'.[4] In resisting class politics, Liberals were standing, not only for a conception of the general interest, but also for the supremacy of mind over matter. Today, in the days of *Sun* Conservatism and champagne Socialism, other parties do not have a class base either and, for the first time since 1918, Liberals can contest elections on a level playing field. It is an exciting opportunity.

When Asquith, in his resignation speech of 1926, gave the reasons for preserving a Liberal party, he picked the rejection of class politics in favour of the interests of the community alongside 'the preservation and extension of liberty in every sphere of our national life' as the two things which justified the continuation of an independent Liberal party.[5] These two forces had a very large part in preventing Labour from swallowing the party up. When another party did manage to appeal to these feelings, it was more often One Nation Conservatives than it was Labour. When I first took a serious interest in the party, in the 1950s, we held one third of our six seats by electoral pacts with the Conservatives and people were saying that we would *always* be the Conservatives' stooges. That was the Conservative Party which drew Ian Gilmour into politics, and it underlines the point made by Alan Beith in 1995, that it is impossible to remain permanently equidistant between two moving points. Those points, of course, have not stopped moving, and in forty years' time our positioning of 1999 may seem as antiquated as our positioning of 1955 does now.

During the wilderness years, it was much harder for the party to identify its distinctive and continuing principles because, as usual, the winners were writing the history. As class politics seemed supreme in electoral terms, so class analysis seemed supreme in academic terms. The decline of Liberalism was presented as an inexorable consequence of the rise of the working class, and any attempt to explain what happened to the Party in the essentially personal terms of the Asquith-Lloyd George quarrel was regarded as a serious symptom of what the *Annalistes* described as *'l'histoire évènementielle'* – mistaking the froth floating on the surface for the power of the current which carried it. The mood, if not its academic underpinnings, was captured in George Dangerfield's *Strange Death of Liberal England*, which has recently been described by G.D. Searle as 'much more of a period piece than the objects of its mockery'.[6] As recently as 1972, John Vincent found it 'strange' that there was a specific working-class dimension in rank and file Liberalism under Gladstone, and dismissed working-class support for the Liberals as 'irrational'.[7] That was not merely patronising: it was an incongruous intrusion of Aristotelian naturalism into a post-Marxian class analysis.

The academic tide began to turn three years before the political, with the publication in 1971 of Peter Clarke's *Lancashire and the New Liberalism*. That book showed the Liberals, taking advantage of the Reform Act of 1885, dropping roots as a party capable of attracting a very large and loyal working-class vote. As Peter Clarke showed in a subsequent article, the party was still gaining votes in by-elections in mining seats right up to 1914. If there was anything inevitable about the rise of the working-class leading to the decline of Liberalism, it does not show up in his evidence.

Since then, there has been a rising flood of serious work on Liberal history, increasingly emancipated from the teleological framework of Labour-influenced historiography of the 1960s. This work has tackled the other point which used to be held to make Liberal decline inevitable: the party's supposed commitment to *laissez-faire*. That remains an article of faith at Westminster, and in what, forty years ago, I would have called 'Fleet Street', but it has been rejected with rare unanimity by the academic community. It is time this rejection was noticed. This issue will be the subject of a separate chapter, but it is worth noting a comment by Anthony Howe, that Free Trade in the age of Lloyd George 'rested fundamentally on different ideological premises from the outmoded Ricardian and evangelical arguments on which the nation had first been drawn to the Free Trade cause'.[8] Free Trade was first of all a campaign for cheap food, and thus was one of the most solid bonds between the Liberal Party and its working-class electorate. Even in the 1840s, Liberals were never a purely *laissez-faire* party, and in the age of Lloyd George, they were probably farther from it than they have been in the age of Paddy Ashdown. The part played by Keynes in finding remedies for unemployment was well within a continuing Liberal tradition, and something in which the party should take pride.

The Liberal Party which entered the twentieth century, like the Liberal Democrats who are leaving it, was well placed to fight Labour, both in terms of electoral resources and in terms of principles and traditions. In 1900, as in 1999, the question was how far we wished to do so. There are at stake here two rival visions of the party and of British politics. In one of these, the party is seen as part of a larger force called 'the centre-left'. The assumption is made that 'progressive' forces must be moving roughly in the same direction, and that, somewhere in the area of commitment to social justice, there is a broad common ground which holds them together. This two-sides, left-right analysis carries with it something of the class-based thinking which has been the hallmark of the twentieth century. In this vision, the Labour government of 1945 is seen as the ideological heir of the Liberal government of 1906.

In the other vision, the party is seen, not just as a 'progressive force', but more specifically, as committed to a deep Liberal philosophy, with its roots stretching back through the nineteenth century to the seventeenth. That vision rejects entirely any notion of a thing called 'the centre-left', and judges the Labour Party by how far it measures up to Liberal principles. The answer, inevitably, is 'not very well', since, however liberal some individual Labour politicians may be, this is something which the Labour Party collectively has never professed or attempted to do.

What is interesting is to see how entrenched both these visions were in party thinking at the beginning of the twentieth century. Sir Henry Campbell-Bannerman, who described the two parties as 'both elements in the progressive forces of the country' and 'going together nine tenths of the way', spoke words Paddy Ashdown could have repeated.[9] By contrast, Asquith in his resignation speech said: 'the appearance of the Labour Party on the scene has done nothing to invalidate, or to render obsolete, the mission of Liberalism. There are no doubt some political and social changes for which we could work side by side with, at any rate, a section of Labour, just as there are some for which we could work side by side with the more progressive and broad-minded among the Conservatives.'[10] These are words Jackie Ballard or Charles Kennedy could have repeated. The words of Councillor Kemp, who said: 'have no more talk about the two wings of a progressive party', and added that if we did not fight them, we 'would be wiped out' could be passed off as the words of our present Councillor Kemp, recently our Leader on Liverpool City Council. They are not: this Councillor Kemp came from Leicester.[11]

The fact that these visions have co-existed in the party for so long suggests that they are not mutually exclusive. The party has lived through the past century by the creative tension between them, and unless or until it becomes clear that Labour is no longer a party of the centre-left, it will no doubt continue to do so. I have myself held both of them at different stages of my life. I was persuaded to the first by the first Home Secretaryship of Roy Jenkins, the first full-blooded believer in the philosophy of John

Stuart Mill to hold that office. I was turned into a passionate adherent of the second by the experience of entering Parliament, and realising the extent of the arrogance of power shown by government. This is not a problem of Tory government, or of Labour government, but of Government of any political complexion. The basic Liberal philosophy of the control of power looks to me far more important, and the chances of relying on any other party to do it far weaker, than I had ever realised. The need for a genuinely Liberal Party now looks to me not merely great, but overwhelming. It is not for nothing that Liberalism has become one of the world's great political philosophies. It is because it met a need, whose depth I had only dimly begun to appreciate.

Whatever balance is next struck between the two visions of the party, it is the second which preserves its distinctiveness as a party, and the second which provides the perspective from which this book is written. It is an attempt to identify, not just the present creed of a party, but the continuity over the centuries in the basic principles of Liberalism. This continuity is often missed because of the distinctive twentieth-century failing of trying to analyse nineteenth-century politics in terms of economics rather than of religion. Professor Biagini is surely right that in the age of Gladstone 'working-class Liberalism was not the fruit of the ideological success of bourgeois ideas during the mid-Victorian decades, but rather the continuation of older and genuinely popular plebeian traditions.' These arose very largely from religion, but in his words: 'these were conflicts about church power, not religious principles.'[12] That is why they provide a grounding in how to apply the Human Rights Act in the twenty-first century. Principles designed to protect Nonconformist Aldermen in the reign of Queen Anne had been translated into principles of racial non-discrimination before the end of the American Civil War. Their application to gender and sexual orientation has taken us a little longer, but in those fields too, we find principles taken from the religious politics of the seventeenth century can be applied to the sexual politics of the twentieth. This approach has given Liberalism a philosophical continuity almost unique in British, and possibly in world, politics.

These basic principles recur like faces in family portraits. Like faces in family portraits, they are never quite the same in two generations, yet the family likeness is plain enough. Like family portraits, they bring in over the generations a steadily wider range of faces with each generation's intermarriage. We have added principles over the centuries by intermarrying them with those we held already, so new principles come in by mixture with the old, and acquire a distinctive Liberal flavour as they do so.

Some of our basic principles go back almost to the very beginning, in 1679. These include the commitment to control and accountability of power, with which it all began. They include the commitments to pluralism and non-discrimination, which have managed to increase and multiply without ever much changing the basic philosophical premises with which they began. Others, such as the commitment to democratic control involved in Parliamentary reform, the commitment to the underdog which was the driving force of nineteenth-century radicalism, and the internationalism we owe to Gladstone, were brought in in the nineteenth century. Mill's commitment to liberty in that wherein we do no harm to others, though it was a nineteenth-century contribution, did not really reach the mainstream of the party until the twentieth century. It is now at the very centre of our thinking. The most recent is the commitment to Green Liberalism, which has come in within my own lifetime. That, like the rest, has been assimilated by feeding it into the mix of ideas which were already familiar.

The chapters of this book, rather than splitting the party up by centuries, will look at these themes in the order in which they came into our thinking. No doubt other challenges will create other additions to this stock of basic principles. The book will end with a survey of some current issues which call for further Liberal thinking, and will ask questions about how the party might respond to them. After 320 years, this is a creed which is still growing.

2

Controlling Executive Power

'We are the only party willing to come into office committed to controlling our own power.' These were the words of Alan Beith, now our Deputy Leader, speaking at the Party Conference of 1991. They are the very heart of what Liberalism is all about. They would be recognised, not just by British Liberals, not just by twentieth-century Liberals, but by Liberals in all countries and in all times as what Oliver Cromwell used to call 'the root of the matter'.

One of the reasons why it is so hard for parties to understand each other is that they have their philosophies about different things. Traditional Conservatism was largely about property. Traditional Socialism was largely about class. Liberalism is and remains largely about power. When we say 'power', we do not just mean the power of the central government. Power, as Grey's 'village Hampden' knew well, may be concerned with petty tyrants as well as great ones, and much of this book will be about controlling non-governmental power. That concern balances, but does not supersede, the traditional concern with controlling the power of government.

Liberals have never been against power. Like sex, it is an elemental force, and we will not survive without it. We have never been, as some of the far Right are, a party of neo-anarchists. We know that a civilised community needs power, and is not safe without it. Power, like sex, should be subject to two restrictions. First, it is unlawful if it does not rest on consent. Second, it is often more enjoyable and more rewarding if it is set in the context of a relationship. The art of Liberalism has never been to destroy power. It has been to set it in the context of these two types of restriction, and thereby to secure a two-way relationship between those who exercise it and those over whom it is exercised. The less categorical the distinction between the governors and the governed becomes, the more Liberal the society in question.

Liberals instinctively recoil at Ernie Bevin's famous definition of Socialism: 'Socialism is what Labour governments do.' Liberal governments, like other governments, are human and have sometimes succumbed to the temptations of power. We do not, like the Pharisee, claim that we are better than other men. It is precisely because we do not that we are so committed to the control of power. We would prefer to think that Liberalism is what Liberal members believe, and that part of their task is to remind Liberal governments of it when they become unduly tempted by power.

Liberalism is like an onion: a series of outer leaves growing tightly round a central heart. This is the heart and, appropriately, it is where the Liberalism of today is closest to the founding Whiggery with which the party began 320 years ago. We cannot claim a continuous loyalty to these principles. Sir Robert Walpole, for example, is not famous for his willingness to reduce his own power. What we can claim is a recurring loyalty to these principles. We keep coming back to them, and in 1999 we are perhaps as close to our founding principles as at any time in our history. This gives us a claim to be regarded as the oldest political party in the world – born 1679, and still going strong. We make Johnny Walker look like a stripling.

This is a big claim, and most of the rest of this book will be devoted to trying to justify it. In institutional terms, we can claim an organizational continuity from the Whigs, formed in 1679 to attempt to exclude James, Duke of York (later James II) from the succession. Their continuous institutional history runs to 1859, when they merged with the Peelites to form the Liberals. The Liberals have a continuous institutional history from 1859 to 1988, when they merged with the Social Democrats to form the Liberal Democrats, who are now the standard bearers for Liberal principles.

We have been great gainers from these two mergers. The merger with the Peelites brought us Gladstone, as the merger with the

Social Democrats brought us his biographer, Roy Jenkins. Both mergers brought us a galaxy of talent and vital experience of office. Yet neither really brought us a philosophy. This is in part because both brought in a top-slicing of the ablest people in the parties they left, but did not bring in a large body of activists. Jonathan Parry is probably right in arguing that in matters of economic policy, Gladstone was fundamentally a Peelite. Yet Gladstone's low-spending, non-interventionist approach to economic policy did not drop root in the party because it clashed with the more radical anti-privilege, anti-monopoly approach of Liberal activists. By 1896, Gladstone himself had read the writing on the wall, and said that he was 'a dead man, one fundamentally a Peel-Cobden man'.[1]

In the merger of 1988, this adherence to a continuing Liberal philosophy was the clearer for the fact that many of the most distinguished figures in the SDP were in philosophical terms already Liberals before they left the Labour Party. Roy Jenkins' first Home Secretaryship, when the philosophy of John Stuart Mill was first applied in office, should rank as one of the great achievements of Liberal government. Bob Maclennan, immediate past President of the Liberal Democrats, is the man who co-ordinated our contribution to the constitutional reform programme in this Parliament, and thereby carried on our commitment to the control of power. He, too, was a Liberal by instinct long before he joined the Liberal Democrats, and this book owes a great deal to his encouragement. Many of the best Liberals in the party come to us through the Social Democrats. Those who were not clearly Liberals when they arrived came suffering from a surfeit of ideology in their previous life in the Labour Party, and were not in a mood to construct any further ideology. Their contribution to the party, and it was a very valuable one, was to add spit and polish, concern with costing, emphasis on the workable, and awareness of the difficulty of translating principle into legislation. That is something for which the party should be profoundly grateful, but it does not in any way weaken our claim to be philosophically a Liberal Party. Tony Greaves, who led the opposition to merger in 1988, but accepted the majority decision when it went against him, said to me in 1996, 'for the first few years, I wasn't sure whether it was going to be a Liberal Party, but now I am sure it is.'[2] If he is sure, who would venture to contradict him?

This is a work of political philosophy, not of short-term political polemic, and it is no part of my purpose to argue about whether the continuing Liberal Party, the small breakaway group led by Michael Meadowcroft, is also a Liberal Party in philosophical terms. I am concerned to assert that the Liberal Democrats are such a party, not that anyone else is not. It is unimaginable to me that the benches on which I was privileged to sit beside Jo Grimond could be thought to be speaking for anything other than Liberalism.

By sheer chance, the chronology of the merger enabled me to embody some of this continuity. In 1988, I was the last person to apply for a Writ of Summons to the House of Lords as a Liberal. When, three months later, I received my Writ and took my seat, I was the first person to enter Parliament as a Liberal Democrat. I was certainly not aware that I stood for any different cause in one capacity from that I had enlisted for in another. Similarly, my great-grandfather, Lord John Russell, was on the platform at the merger of the Whigs and the Peelites. He was twice Prime Minister, once as a Whig and once as a Liberal, and he was certainly not aware that there was any philosophical difference between the creed of his first administration and that of his second. For him, perhaps more than for any other Liberal, the creed of nineteenth-century Liberals was that of the seventeenth-century Whigs, of whom William Lord Russell, the Whig Martyr of 1683, had been such a prominent member. I can still remember, when I was five, looking at William Lord Russell's portrait on the wall, and asking my father what he did. My father replied: 'Oh, he was a *very* good man. The King cut his head off.' The distrust of unfettered power implicit in that remark is very deep in the Liberal inheritance, and very deep in the current Liberal Democrat concern with constitutional reform.

The Whig Party is commonly recognised as having come into existence during the struggles of 1679-81 to prevent the succession of James, Duke of York to the throne. These were, in the short term, unsuccessful, but it took James only three years on the throne to persuade his countrymen that the Whigs had been right.

With the aid of a Dutch army helpfully provided by William of Orange, he was duly excluded from the throne in 1688.

His departure brought the party's first great political thinker, John Locke, back from his exile in Holland. He celebrated his return by the publication of his *Second Treatise of Civil Government*, much of which had probably been written many years before, and of his *Letter Concerning Toleration*. His fellow political thinker Algernon Sidney was not so lucky. He had been executed as part of the reaction against the Whigs in 1683, and his *Discourses* were first published posthumously by John Toland, who is known to have tampered significantly with at least one of the texts he edited. Both men were widely remembered by Victorian radicals for their contributions to Liberal thought.[3]

It should not cause too much surprise that their importance was more obvious to later generations than it had been to their contemporaries. The men of 1688 had to the full the tendency of politicians to try to maximise their support by seeking the middle ground. They therefore insisted that they had not resisted James II or deposed him. Rather, when he threw the Great Seal into the Thames, he had 'abdicated', or, as one of my pupils once put it, 'was abdicated'. That did not save the Whigs for long, for in order to be able to put William and Mary on the throne, they had to assert that it was 'vacant'. The idea that the throne could be vacant had distinct revolutionary implications, for it carried with it the idea that title to power did not rest simply on birth, but on the consent of the governed. That idea had of course to be explicit in the idea of excluding James from the succession in 1679. The Scots, who had a developed idea of popular sovereignty where the English did not, were more explicit, and said in their Claim of Right in 1689 that James had forfeited the government and had been deposed.

For over thirty years, respectable Whigs tried to hide from the implications of what they had done. In 1710, the Bishop of Bath and Wells said that resistance was sometimes necessary, but 'this ought to be kept from the knowledge of the people. The revolution was not to be boasted of, and made a precedent; but we ought to throw a mantle over it, and call it a vacancy or abdication'.[4] As this speech proclaims on its face, such a line could not be held.

Inevitably, it became increasingly clear that the only clear line of defence was that used by Locke, that there was no hereditary title to power, and any right to power rested in the consent of the governed. What is more, it was essential to the defence of 1688, and even more of 1679, to insist that any such title to power was revocable. A government held power on conditions, and if those conditions were broken, its power could be taken away. In Algernon Sidney's words, 'If the multitude therefore do institute, the multitude may abrogate, and they themselves, or those who succeed in the same right, can only be fit judges of the performance of the ends of the institution.'[5] Governments could not be judge and party in their own cause. They could not say 'we know best'. They had to be answerable to their superiors. 1688 committed the Whigs, willy-nilly, to what Professor Walter Ullmann called 'an ascending theory of power'. Power came up from the people, who conferred it on government. Being the ultimate source of authority, they could take away what they conferred.

To modern democrats, all this may appear an unexceptionable series of truisms of no great political significance. Yet from the very beginning, this belief, like many other Liberal principles, was pregnant with possibilities of which most of those who preached it remained blissfully unaware. This possibility occurred to some radical Whigs. John Tutchin maintained that what they had done rested on 'the law of nature, which allowed of no distinctions between persons, all being equal, and it gave the people a natural right to change their rulers.' He went on to assert that 'it is contrary to the nature of any government to have offices hereditary.'[6] In the words of my former pupil, Marina Patrick, it is of the essence of Liberalism to believe in 'equality of birthright'.

Tutchin here asserts a principle which, at the time of writing, has not yet been achieved. We may perhaps leave out the monarchy, which is now not so much an office of government, as returning officer for the Palace of Westminster. No one now proposes that we elect our returning officers as a matter of principle. On the other hand, I must plead guilty to the charge that, as a member of the House of Lords, I am still exercising hereditary political power. Legislation to stop me doing so is in progress. I do not believe that my ancestors intended this when they set the Exclusion Bill in motion in 1679, yet it follows logically from the challenge they then launched to the principle of power based on birth. This is only one example among many of the way an apparently simple general principle, if held firmly and as a central conviction, turns out to have all sorts of implications of which its founders were unaware. Having spent 320 years working through these implications, we would be as unwise to think we have finished as Odysseus was to think he had finished his journey when he returned to Ithaca.

Electoral accountability is not enough to control power. It is not enough to claim we have an ascending theory of power if it comes up from the people once every five years, and then comes down again in a five-year uncontrollable avalanche from Downing Street. The power of the executive must be checked between elections. This was clear enough to Locke, but since he wrote, the executive has acquired control over the legislature. It has learnt to control the body which should control it. This has not always been so. In the years from 1855 to 1865, when the party structure was in temporary confusion, government was defeated in the House of Commons 112 times.[7] One can imagine the outcry which would come from Downing Street if anything like that should happen now. Two developments gave the executive control over the House of Commons. One is the growth of party. The power to deselect a member of Parliament, by denying him his party's nomination at the next election, is in effect a power to sack him – without any compensation for unfair dismissal. That is the stick. The corresponding carrot is the immense growth of government patronage. Between the proliferation of ministerial jobs, the gift of peerages and honours, and the innumerable appointments to government quangos, government possesses a pork barrel of dimensions of which Walpole could only dream.

In the face of this, measures like the abolition of hereditary power are no more than mopping up from old battles of centuries ago. However right, and however necessary, they do not address the needs of today. The Prime Minister has taken over all the powers of the monarchy, through control of patronage and of the Royal Prerogative. Through party, he controls the House of Commons, which used to act as independent critic to the monarchy. Because he enjoys the powers of Parliamentary sovereignty, he can alter the law whenever it inconveniences him. We pride ourselves on our constitutional government, but should we be remembering the remark of Edmund Burke, that 'detestation of past tyranny is consistent with every advantage of present servility'? It is time we realised how frightening an accumulation of power we are subject to.

The danger of this power does not just consist in the danger of oppression. It consists, perhaps equally, in the intellectual sloth which afflicts a government which believes it cannot be substantially checked. Ministers who finish drafting their legislation, like authors who finish writing their books, believe that 'I've done that'. They are, very properly, exhausted, and do not want to do any more revision. If they are not forced to think again, they do not. Rational criticism, even if persuasive, is not enough to overcome exhaustion. Only fear of defeat does that. If fear of defeat is absent, the quality of government falls. Though it undoubtedly did not realise the fact, one of the worst misfortunes the Thatcher government suffered was that it was only defeated in the Commons twice in eleven years. Fear of defeat concentrates the ministerial mind wonderfully.

Accountability is of two kinds: political and legal. Both are equally necessary, and they meet two different kinds of need. Political accountability must deal with gross errors of judgement, unworkably drafted legislation, and measures which cannot be enforced. Legal accountability can deal with gross abuses of power and with breaches of clear legal principles. It cannot deal with plain error.

The 1688 Whigs were aware of both needs. One of the best things they did was the provision in the Bill of Rights that a judge can only be dismissed by an Address carried by a two-thirds majority in both Houses of Parliament. This in effect means that judges can only be dismissed with the consent of the Opposition, and thereby guarantees their independence. This means, in effect, that judges who leave the Bench do so for incompetence, garrulity or sheer capacity to create embarrassment. They do not do so because they are suspected of political bias, however infuriating to the powers that be. On one occasion in the 1950s, the *Observer* carried a leader which said: 'This procedure has never yet been employed. But there are times when it should be.' The judge in question had interrupted counsel 543 times in the course of a single speech. He resigned the following week. There was no prospect of any opposition hailing him as a martyr.

It is only if the judges are independent that we can say, as Algernon Sidney did, that 'the laws of every nation are the measure of magistratical power'.[8] This devotion to the independence of the judiciary has continued unbroken from 1689. In 1993, Nancy Seear, then our Deputy Leader in the House of Lords, said: 'If my party should abandon the independence of the judiciary, I would promptly abandon my party.' This remark had the greater weight for the fact that it came from someone who had unbroken membership of the party for sixty years, and had joined it in the week when Hitler dissolved the Reichstag and took the power to legislate by decree.

The threat to legal control of political power is not now a threat to the independence of the judiciary. It is the power of Parliamentary sovereignty, at the disposal of ministers with a very human dislike of being told they are wrong. In 1996, when Lord Justice Simon Brown quashed the Regulations taking benefit away from asylum seekers, saying it created 'a desolation so great that, in my opinion, no civilised society can suffer it', ministers did not back off. They simply used the panoply of Parliamentary sovereignty to replace the defective Regulations with the full weight of an Act of Parliament. When the Lords threw that measure out, they simply reversed the House of Lords also. This was surely the action of a government constitutionally out of control. It is no use blaming this on one particular party, as subsequent events have shown. It is simply part of the animal government, regardless of its political complexion. Inside all of us, there is a thwarted two-year-old struggling to get out. In ministers whose power is not subject to adequate constitutional checks, it sometimes succeeds.

Measures of this sort, which give a government power to act against a group of people in an arbitrary way, unchecked by legal restraints, can always be counted on to unite the party in opposition to them. It was this reflex, back in the 1950s, which made opposition to compulsory identity cards one of the party's signature tunes when it was at its very lowest ebb. It was the same reflex, in the winter of 1996-7, which united us in opposing police powers to bug private premises without legal checks. On this occasion, the party generated such a head of steam that we succeeded, for the first time in thirty years, in winning a majority in the House of Lords against the wishes of both Government and Opposition Front Benches. This had widely been held to be impossible, and the success in achieving it illustrates the power a small group can have if it is singing a catchy and highly recognisable tune.

Such victories are of course extremely rare. They will not be common until either government defeats in the House of Commons become acceptable, or we have a legal authority proof against the power of Parliamentary sovereignty. Increasingly, for many Liberal Democrats, the first is becoming one of the leading purposes of Proportional Representation. That the governing party (even if it were to become our own) should not enjoy the arbitrary authority of a single-party majority in the House of Commons is increasingly becoming an end in itself. It is to the same end that we are desperately concerned that, when the hereditary principle finally disappears, we should replace it with a Second Chamber capable of inflicting serious defeats on government. A serious case can be made for arguing that this is something we need regardless of what the matter of the defeats might be. Lord Acton was surely right that absolute power corrupts absolutely, and our present government is far too near absolute power for comfort. It is not that we suspect any likely government of deliberate dictatorial intentions: personally, most of them are perfectly reasonable people. They do suffer, like all the rest of us, from the natural human weaknesses of self-will and sloth. Given a system which allows them to get away with having their own way regardless of criticism, they will do so simply because it is the line of least resistance. It is because it forces the government to think twice that the need to bargain and compromise is so essential. I was once chatting to a minister whom I had just helped to defeat in the lobbies, and he said to me: 'All governments must bargain and compromise, and all governments must be defeated in the House of Lords.'[9] The day after this conversation, I was reading a speech by Charles I, in which he said that he could not possibly accept a Parliamentary defeat, because to do so he would have to compromise, and that was wrong. The conjunction of the two remarks makes the point perfectly.

The other alternative method of control, by legal power immune from reversal by Parliamentary sovereignty, at this moment looks slightly more accessible. To many Liberal Democrats, one of the most attractive things about the European Union is precisely what drove Conservative ministers most wild about it: that it subjects British governments to law which an Act of Parliament cannot reverse. In that, it attempts no more than the mediaeval papacy attempted through the medium of canon law. The mediaeval papacy, whatever Pope Boniface VIII may have thought, was not a super-state. It was a system of law, with limited objectives and of limited scope, but whose application was Europe-wide. Like the papacy, the European Union must exercise its power with care and keep it accountable if it wants to preserve it. Yet one may quote such things as the crisis over achieving and keeping Magna Carta to argue that the existence of the power was by no means purely a bad thing.

More immediately, we have the Human Rights Act, which makes it possible for the European Convention on Human Rights to be applied by our judges in our domestic courts, instead of only by international judges in the European Court of Human Rights. This is nothing to do with the European Union: it comes from the Council of Europe, the much larger body which preceded the move to 'ever closer union' started by the Six in 1955. Like the law of the European Union, it has force because Parliament has so provided, and therefore offers no theoretical challenge to the power of Parliamentary sovereignty. Yet at the same time, it will offer a very practical challenge to a great many things Parliament may attempt to do. For example, the Act against terrorism of 1998, which followed the Omagh bombing, provoked an observation from one of the judges. He said that the attempt to convict people of membership of a proscribed organisation on the strength of the opinion of a police officer plus inferences from the silence of the accused would, once the Human Rights Act was in force, instantly be struck down by the Court of Appeal. The Human Rights Act, perhaps alone among the measures of this government, appears to pass Alan Beith's test: they were willing to come into office committed to controlling their own power. Yet the Act has not yet come into force. Liberal Democrats will be much happier when it has done so.

In the long run, there is no way of controlling the potentially arbitrary character of Parliamentary sovereignty short of a written constitution. This is the way of tackling the problem which has been adopted in every liberal democracy save Britain and Israel, and it is in the long term the solution Liberal Democrats want. However, it is clearly not going to happen in the near future, and until it does, there will be no substitute for the proverbial eternal vigilance.

The attempt to remodel the constitution in order to control power, on which the party is now engaged, is not being made for the first time. It follows, not only the burst of constitutional change which was expressed in 1688, but the much more far-reaching series of changes which began in 1832. Those, too, were intended, far more than modern readers usually appreciate as a way of controlling executive power. They were intended to dismantle what twentieth-century idiom might describe as the first quango state, the system of government by patronage so vividly described by Sir Lewis Namier in *The Structure of Politics at the Accession of George III*. Namier's, like so many brilliant works, may have expressed a half-truth, but it was that half which the Whigs of 1832 intended to reverse. Essentially, the Namierite system was one of the use of patronage to allow a ministry to buy a majority in the House of Commons, and to buy a majority in General Elections. The system never worked perfectly, but it could be alarmingly effective. In Sir Lewis's chilling phrase, 'eighteenth-century ministries did not lose elections'. That was not just because of bribery of electors, though that was never absent. It rested on the power of the great borough patrons like the Dukes of Newcastle and Bedford, and on the use of government contracts in dockyard constituencies as well as much else. One way and another, all forms of Government patronage such as church livings, commissions in the Army and appointments to a whole host of obsolete government offices were assembled to the task of winning a government a majority. Criticism was not ruled out: a minister

pursuing an unpopular policy, like Walpole during the Excise
Crisis, might find the price of a majority went up. Yet the task of
controlling a Parliament was not as difficult as it should have
been. In Professor Kenyon's words, the Commons by 1750 were 'a
machine which voted increasingly large sums of money for purposes over which it had diminishing control'.[10]

The Whigs of course had only themselves to blame for this
situation. They had created most of it during their long period of
power during the reigns of the first two Georges, and it was not
until they found it in the hands of the Tories that they began to
understand what was wrong with it. The maxim that 'all power
tends to corrupt' applies to Whigs and Liberals with just as much
force as to anyone else.

The injection of voter power which was offered by the 1832
Reform Bill was not an isolated measure. It was part of a much
larger series of measures designed to restrict the power of money
in politics – a concern which has been with the party ever since. It
is not that we are hostile to the power of money in the market,
provided competition is fair and not rigged. It is that we are hostile
to the power of money *in politics*. If political power depends on
consent, our consents ought to count equal. If one person or group
can buy a political measure by deploying financial strength not
available to the rest of us, there cannot be any reason of political
principle why the rest of us should be bound to consent to it. It is not
often that private money in politics is clearly spent in the general
interest. It is more often spent for competitive reasons, in order to
secure a competitive advantage over those who spend their money
less freely – or less wisely. This rigs the market as well as corrupting
politics. There is no reason why we should put up with it.

The measures of 1832 followed a long attack on obsolete offices.
It was the abolition of one of these, which had been preserved only
for its use to government patronage managers, which led to the
burning of the tally sticks of the Exchequer, which produced the
famous fire which burnt down the Palace of Westminster in 1834.

In the Reform Bill itself, it is not often remembered that the
proposal which produced most outrage was not the extension of the
franchise. It was the principle that constituencies should be re-
drawn to make them roughly proportionate to the number of

voters. It was this which was a head-on onslaught on the principle of what the eighteenth century had liked to call 'electoral property'. It rejected the idea on which Parliament had been founded, that its function was to represent powerful interests, and replaced it with a numerical obligation to represent people. That was the first injection of the notion of proportionality into the electoral system, and it created outrage. Its underlying purposes included the aim of making electorates too large to be bought.

The aim was not of course entirely successful, and it took two further Reform Bills before it was altogether achieved. Over the next generation it was followed by other measures like the introduction of competitive examination in the Civil Service and the abolition of purchase of commissions in the army, which further cut down the power of patronage to control Parliament.

Even the commitment to retrenchment which was so characteristic of early nineteenth-century Liberals was defended because, in Professor Biagini's words, 'keeping the state economical was a crucial means of constitutional control'. This case was the easier to argue because the bulk of public expenditure was not for the benefit of the common people, but on things like army, navy, police, diplomatic service and Civil List, 'which, as the late Mr Cobden very pithily expressed it, "have for their real object the granting of outdoor relief for the younger sons, poor relations and favourites of the aristocracy".' In the light of this point, the change in the party's attitude to public spending between the party of Gladstone and that of Lloyd George and Ashdown may not be as big an ideological shift as it is sometimes portrayed as being.[11]

Right from the very beginning, the party also limited power by controlling the ends for which it could be legitimately exercised. This does not begin with Mill *On Liberty*: it begins with Locke's *Letter Concerning Toleration*. By proposing to restrict the purposes of the State to preserving the civil interests of its subjects, rather than concerning itself with their salvation, he erected a large roadblock between the state and the individual conscience. He also produced a powerful limit on the degree of uniformity a state was able to attempt to impose. A state based on religious toleration had a crucial commitment to diversity and a crucial restriction in its purposes. When Locke argued for toleration of the

Mass on the ground that 'if a Roman Catholic believes that to be really the Body of Christ, which another man calls bread, he does no injury thereby to his neighbour',[12] he exactly anticipated Mill's test of liberty in that wherein we do no harm to others. Professor Biagini has pointed out that this commitment to ideological diversity, and to a degree of separation of church and state, made a crucial difference to the quality of Liberal patriotism. In his words, 'they saw religion as a matter of personal choice rather than of group or national allegiance.' Because they were able to conceive of a degree of separation between church and state, they had a less uniform concept of nationalism, and less authoritarian tendencies than those who believed in one faith, one law and one King.[13] That was an immense asset when they came to consider the relations between England and Britain, and helped to make possible the approach to the control of power by dispersal which will be one of the central themes of the next chapter.

Some readers who have read this far will undoubtedly ask what is distinctive about all this. They will say these are things every serious politician now believes, and that the chapter deals with nothing but motherhood and apple-pie. If so, they will have failed to observe that a good many Americans do not actually like motherhood and apple-pie.

Before I had the experience of going into Parliament, I might have had some sympathy with these criticisms. I can still remember when I thought that basic liberal values were the stock-in-trade of all politics, rather than an issue which served to divide the parties. When I listen to Willie Whitelaw, Roy Jenkins and Jim Callaghan uniting to attack Michael Howard, I can see why I once thought this. Yet it is a view which grossly underestimates the temptations of power, and especially the pressure to cut corners because of the sheer pressure of work. While other parties may notice and condemn this tendency, there is no other party for which checking such abuse of power is the central purpose of its existence. There is no other which will collectively give the need to control power quite as high a priority as we do. That is one of the most important reasons why, if we did not exist, it would be necessary to invent us.

This is our starting point, our bedrock and our unifying principle. It has been our prime concern over the past ten years, and will be so again. Yet we have many other guiding principles, and at this moment, there are voices in the party which say we ought to increase the priority we give to some of the others. Those voices deserve a hearing. Nikita Khrushchev may have been right that 'if people have to choose between freedom and goulash, they will choose goulash'. Liberals must never forget the goulash.

3

Pluralism

I. The Dispersal of Power

When a Liberal speaks of pluralism, he or she will probably be talking about two ideas which, to a non-Liberal ear, are very clearly distinct. One of these is the attempt to control power by dispersal, a rejection of the notion of the unitary omnicompetent sovereign state so beloved of Thomas Cromwell, in favour of a Russian egg model of political power, in which it is held in a series of containers, one inside another, ranging from the United Nations at one end down to the parish council or an individual family at the other.

The other thing we mean by 'pluralism' is a cult of diversity, religious, social, geographical and cultural, in which 'the old Whig cry of "equality before the law" ' is invoked to defend the rights of the under-privileged, whoever they may happen at that time to be.[1]

The interesting and intriguing question is why we so instinctively assume that these two are part of the same belief. I believe the answer to this conundrum is historical. Both of these go back to our origins, to our commitment to equal rights for Nonconformists against the claims to monopoly privilege of the Church of England. It is at the heart of our identity that this fact does not mean we were ever a Nonconformist party. Until religion ceased to be a subject on which political statistics were normally kept, the Liberals and the Whigs before them at all times had a majority of Anglicans among their leaders, and possibly among their members also. The point is that these were Anglicans who wanted to be able to compete on equal terms with Noncomformists, rather than sheltering behind a tariff barrier of legal privilege.

The argument of the Nonconformists and their friends was not about religion: it was at all times about legal privilege, equality of opportunity, and resistance to the exercise of political power which was not derived from consent. This remained true at all times from the struggles over Occasional Conformity in the reign of Queen Anne down to the abolition of religious tests for university education and the campaign for Nonconformists to be buried in churchyards which launched the career of Lloyd George.

The seventeenth-century rejection of a Tory view which saw church and state as coterminous freed the party to embrace a looser definition of nationality, a less singular definition of power, and a more diverse view of community than the Tory inheritance allowed them to do with any great ease. The rejection of a close church-state identification which was one of the central Whig causes against the Tories in the reign of Anne allowed the party from the beginning to think of power as having more than one centre and as being of more than one type. From the beginning, politics for the Whigs was secular.[2]

At the same time, this championship of a group the party saw as underprivileged gave the party a concern for diversity and a championship of the underdog which have never since left it. The issue was not religious: it was political. In Professor Biagini's words: 'These were conflicts about church power, not religious principles. ... Liberty, civil and religious, included both the Nonconformist and secularist crusades for equality before the law and the Trade Union struggles for a more equal law.'[3] With the irony of true consistency, the same principles enabled us to speak out against Trade Unions when they claimed 'special privileges under the law', of the sort that we had not allowed to 'landlords or churches'.[4] The commitment to equality before the law is consistent, regardless of which 'side' it may put us on for the time being.

This, perhaps, is the common ground which makes us so instinctively identify the two types of pluralism as part of a single creed. This commitment to pluralism certainly enabled Whigs, from the beginning, to accommodate themselves much more easily than the Tories to the British dimension of politics after 1707. The task was not difficult: the Act of Union of 1707 presented the party with an immediate and welcome increase in its majority.

The British dimension was far more difficult for the Tories. The Tories were by their own definition the party of the Church of England, and in Queen Anne's reign 'the church in danger' was one of their regular rallying cries. They were also committed by this attachment to a much tighter identification of church and nation than Whigs ever countenanced. A spoof set of Tory election expenses from Queen Anne's reign included a payment of forty shillings to 'roarers of the word "church" '. If the Church of England, as wags said, was 'the Tory party at prayer', what was the Tory Party in Scotland and Wales?

The Church of England was established in Wales until the Asquith government disestablished it, provoking F.E. Smith to the hyperbolic claim that they had 'shocked the conscience of every Christian community in Europe'. Yet the Anglican church in Wales was never a deeply popular church. It was a church of the governing Welsh gentry, Oxford-educated, Justices of the Peace, Members of Parliament, and as anglicised in their life as in their religion. Extension of the franchise in the nineteenth century led to the return of a mass of Dissenter-born Liberal MPs for whom Lloyd George became a spokesman.

Scotland had an established church which Tories would have regarded, with Anglocentric logic, as Dissenting. The Church of Scotland was and remains a Presbyterian Church based on an ascending theory of power – hardly a fertile ground for Toryism. It was a thorn in the side of English Tories right down to Margaret Thatcher's famous Sermon on the Mound in Edinburgh, when she addressed the General Assembly on the error of their ways. This diversity created no difficulty for Whigs or for Liberals. For Tories right through the nineteenth century, Scotland and Wales were the places which prevented their recurring majorities in England from being translated into majorities at Westminster.

It was Ireland, not Scotland or Wales, which first made Liberals think in terms of breaking up the power of the Imperial Parliament at Westminster. The case put by the Irish Nationalist leader John Redmond was so familiar that it was irresistible to what

Martin Pugh once described as 'Gladstone's ... laboriously acquired Liberalism'. Redmond said:

> I mean by Home Rule the restoration to Ireland of representative government, and I define representative government to mean government with the constitutionally expressed will of a majority of the people, and carried on by a ministry constitutionally responsible to those whom they govern. In other words, I mean that the internal affairs of Ireland shall be regulated by an Irish Parliament.[5]

For Gladstone, there was no incompatibility between the belief that Ireland was a nation, and the belief that Britain was a state. His nationalism was not that of Woodrow Wilson, and for him the union of Austria and Hungary, with two separate legislatures, was a perfectly acceptable parallel. He saw the nationalism of Ireland, like that of Scotland and Wales, as perfectly compatible with membership of the United Kingdom. Whether, if Gladstone had been given his way, he would have proved to be right, or whether it was already too late for this type of solution, is something we will now never know.

Gladstone himself accepted the extension of his ideas to Scotland, but not as a high priority and though bills were introduced for Scottish devolution, they never completed their passage. What brought the issue of Scottish devolution to a head in the 1990s was the same theme which brought the issue of Irish Home Rule to a head in the 1880s. After the Reform Bill of 1884 enlarged the Irish franchise to enfranchise a Catholic Nationalist majority, it seemed that every election would return a majority in the United Kingdom for a party which enjoyed no consent in Ireland. Similarly, the almost total failure of Thatcherism to secure any consent in Scotland seemed to raise a prospect of Scotland being perpetually governed by an alien creed which enjoyed no consent there. It was perhaps natural that the Secretary of State for Scotland acquired the colonial nickname of 'the Governor General'. Both situations put the Whig-Liberal principle of government by consent under intolerable strain. To those for whom it created no philosophical difficulty, devolution seemed an obvious answer.

Scotland enjoys one other peculiarity which Wales and Northern Ireland do not. It has its own separate indigenous system of law. In 1604, James VI and I's Commissioners For the Union decided that the two systems could not be merged. This decision was probably correct: they had different terminologies and concepts, and the task of translation in a possible merger might have been insuperable. Moreover, Scotland had had no equivalent of the English Statute of *Quia Emptores* of 1290, which had effectively turned feudal tenures into a dead letter. The feu duty is at the heart even of present-day Scottish land law, and I have seen the eyes of members of the Westminster Parliament glaze over when they had to deal with it. They would not be competent to handle an Act superseding it.

From one point of view, this strengthens the case for Scottish devolution. It provides what has been the central principle of the Scotland Act, that the power to make Scottish law resides in the Scottish Parliament, and the power to make United Kingdom law resides in the Parliament of the United Kingdom. This is a distinction which has the merit of simplicity. There is surely also force in the point made by Lord Kilbrandon, chairman of the Royal Commission on the Constitution which considered devolution in the 1970s: 'It would be hard throughout the familiar world to find a parallel for a country which had its own judicature and legal system, its own executive and administration, but no legislature, its laws being made within another and technically foreign jurisdiction, by an assembly in which it had only a small minority of members, but to which its executive was democratically responsible.'[6]

The point about the small minority of members is well taken, since it gives perspective to Tam Dalyell's famous West Lothian question. That question asks what right the member for West Lothian has to make English law to which he will not be subject. It is a fair question, but it is no more fair than the West London question we should have been asking for years. By what right does an Englishman living in West London have a right to make Scottish law to which he will not be subject? We have been doing that for years, and only those who have complained of the one thing have a right to complain of the other.

So long as we retain a Union Parliament while having two systems of law, one thing or the other must happen. The question is which is the less unacceptable. It must surely be more acceptable to have Scots making English law, which they cannot do without the assent of some 250 English and Welsh members, than to have Englishmen making Scots law, which they can do, and have done, without the assent of any Scots at all.

The only way out of this choice would be a fully federal system. However, as Montenegro is at present learning, there are severe difficulties in the federation of two units of greatly unequal size. That is why Andrew Fletcher of Saltoun, in the negotiations leading up to the Act of Union, wanted a federal solution based on the regionalisation of England. Such a solution would cause no problems to Liberal Democrats. The difficulty is that English consent to such a solution would be required, and it does not yet appear to be available. Until it is, we should not take West Lothian too seriously. The practical difficulties involved in devolution are legion, and many of them still ahead. Yet in a book which is concerned to set out a party philosophy, there should not be too heavy a concentration on details of policy which may be ephemeral. It is hard, moreover, to resist the suspicion that tackling these difficulties is largely a matter of finding the requisite political will. Most of them consist of apparent illogicalities in arrangements for devolution, especially for its finance. Yet it is not easy to pretend that present arrangements are perfectly logical, nor even to argue a case for saying that if they did not at present exist, we would have adopted them. For Liberals and Liberal Democrats, that political will is there, and the work is being done. It is part of a pluralist view of politics which we have always held.

We can say the same for our commitment to the European Union, which arises from a very similar pluralist approach to power. Indeed, it is probably not a coincidence that Jo Grimond, the leader who committed us to Europe even before the Treaty of Rome, was a Scot, and one who saw Scottish politics from the ultra-pluralist perspective of the Orkney Islands, to which Edinburgh, not London, is the encroaching centre.

We have always known that, as Professor Biagini put it, 'the United Kingdom was neither a nation state nor interested in becoming one. It was a rather archaic multinational state.'[7] We know, as a British party, that we belong to a state which is a result of a pooling of sovereignty and a highly successful currency union. When Margaret Thatcher said that no state could ever accept a pooling of sovereignty, she laid herself wide open to the question whether she was going to join the Scottish Nationalists to introduce a Bill to repeal the Act of Union. England before 1603 was a more or less unitary nation state. Britain has never been one. We know that what the Conservatives are so terrified of losing is something we have not had since 1603, and we seem to have coped well enough without it.

We thus have no conceptual difficulty with membership of the European Union. We know, too, that in the modern world large numbers of questions such as acid rain or the pollution of the Rhine need to be addressed, but cannot be tackled within the limits of national sovereignty. The issues created by the decline of the nation state as an instrument of economic control, because many of them are yet in the future, will be addressed in the last chapter of this book. Because we have always believed in the dispersal of power, such questions cause us no conceptual difficulty.

Yet we are very far from being starry-eyed admirers of everything the European Union does, and this fact would be far more apparent if the Conservatives did not continually attack it on the one ground on which we are constantly compelled to defend it. I can recall Laura Grimond describing the Berlaymont, headquarters of the European Commission, as 'a symbol of everything Liberals ought not to stand for'. It is a vast bureaucracy, inadequately accountable for its spending, and legislating by decree with very little check from the European Parliament.

As the recent call for the resignation of the Commission illustrates, the proper body to hold the Commission to account is the European Parliament. A European-wide Commission can only be held to account by a Europe-wide elected body. The alternative system, of having it held to account severally by fifteen individual member states, is a proposal for a Polish Diet, in which every member has a veto. It simply cannot work, as General de Gaulle, during the period of the famous Empty Chair, came very near proving.

One cannot hold a body accountable without accepting its right to exist. This is an elementary truism which Eurosceptics seem unable to grasp, but it was illustrated by the prominence of the Liberal group in the attack on the Commission during last winter. Because they accepted the existence of a Europe-wide authority, they had no difficulty in attempting to develop a power of Europe-wide control. Conservatives attempting to control European bureaucracy suffer the same handicaps as Scottish Nationalists trying to control British bureaucracy. The job cannot be done that way.

Liberals have always been aware that different powers are appropriately exercised on different levels. Though we see that many macro-economic powers have to be exercised on a supra-national level or not at all, our instinctive preference has always been for devolving power downwards whenever possible, for re-turning power towards the people who are its source. The Liberal state perhaps works best of all when it can, as it has done over education, act as an enabler to give people an opportunity to do what they themselves choose.

Commitment to the autonomy of local government was one of the causes which first drew the party together in the seventeenth century. One of James II's most unpopular measures was his imposition of the Three Questions on Justices of the Peace and Lords Lieutenant. These were designed to commit them to work-ing for the return of Parliamentary candidates who would support the repeal of the Test Act. Those who gave the wrong answers to the questions were dismissed.

In resisting this, the party was working with the grain of English society. It is one of the historical peculiarities of England that it has always enjoyed a very high degree of autonomy in local government. Justices of the Peace in the counties, Mayors and Aldermen in the boroughs and select vestries in the parishes have been the most important people in their local communities, not outsiders sent in to impose royal control. This system, of which the constable, the churchwardens and jurymen were sometimes used as symbols, was one of local self-government, or, as F.W. Maitland felicitously put it, 'self-government at the King's command'. It is this tradition which did much to produce the 'active citizens' so essential to a Liberal vision of society. It was one of the points in which the English most often compared themselves favourably to the continent. In J.S. Mill's words, 'In France everything was done *for* the people, and nothing *by* the people.'[8]

It was in the nineteenth century that this commitment to autonomous local government began to turn into a commitment to elected local government. The Municipal Corporations Act of 1835 followed hard upon the 1832 Reform Bill. This was meant to deal with the evil of borough-mongering which had been part of the machinery for control of the House of Commons, and with the old Whig grievance of the exclusion of Dissenters. It was also, in Lord Melbourne's words, designed to create a 'community of feeling' between the different classes in the towns. In the process, it brought in numbers of anti-slavery campaigners campaigning against the vested interests of oligarchic beneficiaries of the slave trade. It was also meant to deal with the large debts built up by the mismanagement of irremovable urban oligarchies, and modern Liberal Democrats may feel a sense of *déjà vu* at the discovery that Liverpool, when the old regime went out, had accumulated debts of £792,000.[9] In 1885, this was followed by the creation of County Councils, and Hartington, not the party's most dangerous radical, proclaimed that 'the extension of popular self-government all over the country' was a firm Liberal principle.[10]

Liberal suspicion of the growth of the state was not extended to the growth of local government. Much nineteenth-century reforming legislation in such fields as public health took the form of enabling legislation for local government, and that legislation was put to good use. In Professor Biagini's words: 'In fact Gladstone's financial strictness was compatible both with non-expensive forms of state legislation (like factory legislation), and with an expanding scope for local government, the responsibilities and budget of which continued to grow throughout his Parliamentary career.'[11] This approach was not just used for monolithic local authorities. In Sunderland in 1876, a population of 112,000 produced twenty different assemblies, all elected, with 362 representatives.[12] The School Boards introduced under Forster's Education Act were also elected, and were the first body for which women were allowed to vote.

This underlines the fact that nineteenth-century Liberalism was not just a creed of individuals: it was a creed of communities. It was the working of these overlapping communities, some civic, some religious, which made it possible for Liberalism to become so clearly a cross-class creed. A German miner, visiting Newcastle in 1890, commented in surprise that 'the middle- and working-classes were on very familiar terms, because they were brought together in clubs and religious organisations'.[13] The importance of this to the ideal of the Liberal active citizen, ready to involve himself in public life and concern himself (or herself) with the welfare of others is incalculable.

That ideal is of the essence of Liberalism. How we keep it alive in an age when the commonest leisure pursuit is the utterly passive one of television-watching is one of the biggest challenges which face us. It is not insuperable. Concern with public issues has not disappeared, as is shown by the fact that the Royal Society for the Protection of Birds now has more members than all the political parties put together. The problem of creating active citizens in the age of television is one which needs more thought than we have yet given it.

II. Equality

Few themes more rapidly produce misunderstanding than a discussion of equality between a Liberal and an Old Labour supporter. I do not enter into the question what happens in a discussion of equality between a Liberal and a New Labour supporter: as Mao Tse-Tung said when asked the effects of the French Revolution: 'It is too early to say.' The misunderstanding with the Old Labour supporter will be because we are discussing two different things under a single name.

The Old Labour supporter will be concerned with a change in the economic balance between classes, and will be thinking first and foremost of money, and of groups. The Liberal will be thinking of rights and of opportunities, and will be thinking primarily of individuals. To Liberals, as to the American Civil

Rights movement, equality is first and foremost a form of non-discrimination.

This does not mean that, in Samuel Smiles style, we hold people responsible for their own misfortune. From the very beginning, we have married a concern with non-discrimination with a strong and passionate identification with the underdog. In the nature of the case, this is an easy enough identification to make, and three centuries of political campaigning have done nothing but strengthen it. In the second place, we have had from the beginning a firm commitment to the doctrine of the level playing field, as it is now known. A commitment to competition must carry with it a commitment, based on what John Locke called the law of nature and the nineteenth-century called fair play, to the proposition that competition should be fair. If we find one group of people less successful in competition than the others, we ask instinctively whether the playing field is in any way tilted against them. We ask, in particular, whether the group in question have suffered from inequalities of power or of opportunity. Finding someone still unfortunate, we remember the basic commitment to do as you would be done by, and aim to treat them as we would want to be treated in the same situation. It is a very different commitment to equality from Labour's, but we would like to think it has achieved at least as much. It certainly goes more with the grain of treating people as individuals, and helping them to do what they themselves choose to do. We are certain it has done more for liberty, and that is one of the reasons why we believe it has done more for equality. Inequality, after all, may be of power as well as of property.

Ironically, the rhetoric of our Tory opponents at the very beginning made a considerable contribution to this civil rights blend. Professor Kenyon pointed out that Tory sermon attacks on Dissenters on 30th January, when they commemorated the execution of Charles I, betrayed 'an acute class consciousness'. One in 1694 accused Dissenters of believing in 'servants on horses, and princes walking as servants on the earth'. They associated the heroes of the Whig pantheon with this condemnation, and another damned to the pit of Hell 'all our Knoxes, Buchanans, Miltons, Baxters, Sidneys, Lockes and the like agents of darkness'.[14] If this sort of charge is made against people for long enough, they begin to glory in it. It may have done more than we will ever know to turn Sidneys and Russells into stronger champions of the poor and the excluded than they would ever have become without it.

The potentially democratic implications of championship of Dissent were strengthened by the democratic implications of much Dissenting ecclesiology. Congregationalists, for example, believed, in Locke's words, that 'a church is a voluntary society'. Power in such societies rested with the body of their own members, not with any appointed hierarchy. The indefinite article made an equally revolutionary claim to equal civil status with other churches. Both lead on to acceptance of Rainborough's famous remark at Putney in 1947, quoted in 1959 by Jo Grimond as one of his 'liberal texts': 'The poorest he that is in England hath a life to live as the greatest he.'[15] The irony, of course, is that this, one of the great anti-discrimination texts of all time, asserts the principle with one word which is blatantly discriminatory on the face of it. It illustrates the fact that Liberals have been dreadfully slow to recognise the possibilities with which their own principles were pregnant. This has happened often enough for us to be expected to learn from it, and we should perhaps be asking whether, as Gladstone and Asquith were blind to the discriminatory implications of the word 'he', there may be other equally important implications of the principle of non-discrimination to which we are equally blind. That is the sort of self-critical question Liberals must at all times be prepared to ask.

The basic thrust of the principle appears very clearly in the Llanfrothen burial case of 1888, which launched the career of Lloyd George on the warpath. It was a long-standing grievance of Nonconformists that in many places, especially rural parishes with only one graveyard, there was nowhere for them to be buried with their own rites. An Act of Parliament of 1880 met this grievance by allowing them to be buried in parish churchyards with their own rites. Lloyd George's clients, the family of a Dissenting quarryman, tried to bury the quarryman in the churchyard under this Act, and found that the Rector had locked the gates against them. Lloyd George, the family solicitor, advised them to go ahead and conduct the burial without the Rector's permission. The family were prosecuted, and won the case.

To anyone who knows Llanfrothen, it is clear that the graveyard is a natural monopoly. Between rocky ground on one side, and wet ground on the other, there is simply nowhere else bodies could be buried. The issue was discriminatory access to an essential monopoly public service. It is the same issue as in the bus boycott which did so much to start the Civil Rights movement in the American Deep South, and we should not let the fact that one issue is apparently religious and the other apparently secular blind us to their essential similarity.

Certainly nineteenth-century Liberals showed an impressive capacity to universalise the issue of 'civil and religious liberty', rather than letting it hide in sectarian exclusiveness. The acid test of this was the determination of the first Gladstone ministry to disestablish the Anglican church of Ireland. That church, of course, had a very slender popular base in an overwhelmingly Roman Catholic country, and Roman Catholics would be the main beneficiaries of its disestablishment. Party activists were being asked to choose between civil and religious liberty on one hand, and hostility to Rome on the other. They chose unambiguously in favour of civil and religious liberty.

Lord John Russell had a rather harder time when he set out to secure the right of Jews by religion to be returned to the House of Commons. There was no difficulty for converted Jews such as Disraeli, for they could take the Christian oath which was the gateway to membership. Lionel de Rothschild, when he was elected for the City of London in 1847, was not so fortunate. Because he could not take the oath, he was found incapable of membership. Lord John Russell introduced a Jewish Disabilities Bill to remove this obstacle, but had to introduce it in twelve consecutive sessions before he succeeded in getting it on the statute book.

A much bigger storm arose over Charles Bradlaugh, who was elected to the House of Commons in 1880, and denied the right to take his seat because, as a conscientious atheist, he would not take the Christian oath. Gladstone correctly identified the issue of principle, and supported Bradlaugh's claim to take his seat. Lord

Randolph Churchill, in a gross rejection of the principles of pluralism, claimed that this proved Gladstone was an atheist. It was only after a long battle that the right to affirm was created, and Bradlaugh was able to take his seat.

The extension of the principle to race had been accepted and understood, at least by some Liberal activists, before the end of the American Civil War. In this case it was Gladstone, who at first showed an alarming tendency to sympathy with the south, who did not understand the implications of his principles. On the other hand, John Wilson of the Durham Miners' Association, a dedicated Liberal activist, praised Lincoln for not trimming for the sake of a second term in office: 'Equality and the love of human right and a recognition of the fundamental truth that the colour of the skin ought not to differentiate the human race weighed much more with him.'[16] Here, too, the British dimension may have helped. Indeed, on at least one occasion it fused the issues of religion and race. One of the rare occasions when I have felt any twinge of sympathy for Kitchener was the occasion during the First World War when Lloyd George discovered that he was refusing to allow Nonconformist chaplains, and refusing to let Welsh soldiers speak Welsh in their billets. Kitchener had no idea what an elemental force he had taken on, and retreated in bad order.[17]

This story helps to understand Professor Biagini's remark that 'in some areas – notably Wales – the rights of labour and the cause of religious freedom seemed closely intertwined'. Indeed, for many of them, it was religion which gave them the courage and the self-esteem to speak up for the under-privileged. Joseph Arch of the Agricultural Labourers' Union, a future Liberal MP, said his career in Trade Unionism began when he became convinced that he was one of the Elect. George Edwards, an illiterate farm labourer when he was converted, taught himself to read, became a Methodist lay preacher, and searched the Scriptures before devoting himself to Trade Unionism. It was this same creed of non-discrimination which enabled radicals to attack budgets for taxing people for the benefit of a class, or to attack 'the pack of howling ravenous coroneted wolves' in the House of Lords. On the 1871 Trade Union bill, the Trade Unions ran their campaign for amendments under the slogan of 'equality before the law'.[18]

The party may have done an outstanding job of recruiting working-class activists. It was much less successful at electing working-class MPs. In the 1890s, Liberal Associations rarely selected working-class candidates except in two member seats. Present-day Liberal Democrats who defend list systems of election as a way of getting more women MPs may be forgiven a weary smile of recognition. It makes it doubly unfortunate that the move to single member constituencies from 1885 encouraged the drift to class politics. It was not for lack of good candidates coming forward. Keir Hardie, Ramsay MacDonald and Arthur Henderson all applied unsuccessfully for nomination as Liberal candidates. Seldom can a party have suffered so severely for failure to apply its principles in practice.

The party was even slower to react to the case for removing the legal disabilities of women. The first proposal to give them the vote came from John Stuart Mill in 1867. He moved an amendment to the Second Reform Bill, to delete the word 'man' and replace it with the word 'person'. From then, it was fifty-one years until the first women got the vote, and sixty-one years until they got it on equal terms. As a triumph for the Principle of Unripe Time, this takes some beating.

The case made by Millicent Garrett Fawcett, writing in the collection of essays on *Why I Am A Liberal*, in 1885, so exactly captures one of the continuities of Liberalism before and since that it is worth reproducing almost in full.

No section of the people has ever been excluded from political power without suffering legislative injustice. To mention only a few instances: the working-classes suffered for centuries from laws which attempted to fix the rate of wages, to prevent labourers migrating from place to place in search of better-paid employment, to suppress trade societies, and to facilitate the embezzlement of their funds. Women have suffered, and are still suffering, from a number of unjust laws. A mother, if she is married, has no right to the guardianship of her children, and no right, after they have passed an early age, even to be with them. If her husband is unfaithful to her, the law

gives her no claim to a divorce, although infidelity on her part
gives her husband the right to put her away. ...

Every case of injustice is a double curse, harming those it
is supposed to favour, as much as those to whom it is obvi-
ously oppressive; and liberalism, notwithstanding the
timidity of some faint-hearted and weak-kneed Liberals, is
the main force in the political world which cuts at the root of
injustice ... Equal justice to all, man or woman, workman or
aristocrat, is the only sort of liberalism that deserves the
name.[19]

Modern Liberal Democrats will have no difficulty in recognising
those words, in their capacity to universalise a grievance in
terms of a timeless ideal, as expressing the creed we know as
'Liberalism'.

By contrast, the voices of Gladstone and Asquith are painful.
Gladstone claimed that 'a permanent and vast difference of type
has been imposed on women and men respectively by the maker of
both'. Asquith, adopting the voice of Aristotle, said that while
Liberalism attacked unearned or artificial privileges, it should not
interfere with those imposed by 'nature herself'.[20] Those voices do
have a message for modern Liberals. It is that Homer nods, and no
one is a Liberal all the time. That is why power, even if it is our
own, must always be distrusted. A further message most modern
Liberal Democrats would hear is that, until men and women can
compete on a level playing field (and we are not there yet) we will
not know what has, and what has not, been imposed by 'nature
herself'. It is, then, a proper Liberal humility to arrange affairs to
help women to make effective whatever choices they make for
themselves rather than to use the panoply of legislation to impose
a Procrustean pattern where we have neither the understanding
nor the authority to do so. With that thought in mind, we might
reflect on the remark made by Harriet Taylor right at the beginning of the struggle, that if women had been intended only for
domesticity, it would not have been necessary to erect so many
obstacles to exclude them from other roles.[21]

The more politically defenceless any section of the community
may be, the more they stand in need of this claim to non-discrimi-

nation. The greater the weakness, the more urgent the claim to legal equality. One of the most powerful statements of the creed was in an unsigned article in *Reynolds's News* in 1870, attacking the Contagious Diseases Act. That Act was one of those cases which divide Liberal from Liberal, on which Liberal philosophy can be invoked on both sides of the argument. The Act gave the Police the power to impose health checks on prostitutes in garrison towns, and to detain prostitutes *or suspected prostitutes* to that end. It was possible to defend the Act on the pure Millite ground of preventing harm to others, though it was noteworthy that Mill himself was among those who condemned it. It was equally possible to argue, as this article did, that it was discriminatory legislation visiting special penalties on a defenceless section of the community:

> All exceptional laws are objectionable, and none more so than those which give the police exceptional powers over the liberties and persons of the defenceless portion of the community ... Assuredly, this violation of an Englishwoman's person, never mind in how low scale of life she may move, no matter what her mode of life may be, is a monstrous and abominable outrage upon the first principles of liberty, of decency, and of propriety. The person of a prostitute should be as sacred from harm or touch as that of a duchess, or of the Queen herself.

This is pure Liberal principle, and, *mutatis mutandis*, I could repeat the whole line of argument against the proposal to take social security benefits away from asylum seekers. It is indeed 'based on the old Whig cry of "Equality before the law" '. That cry is no less urgent today than it was in 1679.[22]

These ideas are back in fashion today. In the past thirty years, much of the cutting edge of the equality debate has shifted from issues of class to issues of race and gender. Even if we leave out issues of equal rights, and look simply at crude economic inequalities, those two grounds of discrimination probably do as much to produce economic inequality as class does. The institutions which are now at the cutting edge of fighting inequality are the Commission for Racial Equality and the Equal Opportunities

Commission, backed up by the Human Rights Act. All of these rest on an absolutely traditional Liberal philosophy of non-discrimination. In all of these cases, we owe a debt to the Home Secretaryship of Roy Jenkins, and to the continuing influence of those who came into government with him. Once again, the contributions of Roy Jenkins and his circle to the party have not been in bringing in any new philosophy, but in reconnecting it with ideas taken from the Liberal mainstream, cross-pollinated in America, and now urgently needed for use in the political front line. We cannot, thank God, claim to be alone in these ideas, but we are at home in them and ready to use them.

The latest place where the party, on a free vote basis, is applying these ideas is the campaign for legal equality for homosexuals. This is a straight issue of discrimination, as is shown by the outrage of those on the other side of the argument whenever it is suggested that equality is appropriate. Lord Habgood, the former Archbishop of York, once asked us during a House of Lords debate what are the grounds on which it is appropriate for the state to discriminate. It was a fair question, and deserves a fair answer.

In terms of employment, it is appropriate to discriminate in terms of any quality which is essential to doing the job. Among applicants for the job of bus driver, it is appropriate to discriminate in terms of eyesight. The case for discriminating in terms of hearing, though it can be made out, is much more difficult. The case for discriminating in terms of race, gender, social origin or sexual orientation is non-existent. The Equal Opportunities Commission once decided that it was legitimate discrimination not to employ a man for the job of fitting women's bras. If he had appropriate experience, it would be improper discrimination to refuse to employ him for a job involving childcare.

Where employment is not concerned, the appropriate test is Mill's, whether the activity concerned does direct and assignable harm to others. What two young men of seventeen do in bed in private is nothing to do with me, but if they then play their stereo so loud that I cannot continue to write this book, that is something to do with me. It does direct and assignable harm, not only to me, but to the legitimate expectation of my publishers that I will complete the book on time.

The distinction is perfectly straightforward, though, like most clear principles, it will throw up hard cases in the detail of its application. What it does achieve is the total separation of any case for prohibition from the personal moral disapproval of those who would wish to prohibit. In this, it is a late, possibly the last, stage in the separation of religion from politics which we began in the seventeenth century. Government, as Locke insisted, is for the preservation of our civil interests.

It would be unfair to leave this subject of non-discrimination without a word of praise for Paddy Ashdown, who in this area has perhaps been the most courageous and clear-sighted leader we have had. Faced with attacks on an Asian take-away in his own constituency in Yeovil, he had the plain gut Liberal reaction that 'this is wrong', and went out on patrol with the Vicar to stop it. The racist who put a knife to his throat did not know what he had taken on. Paddy had this same gut reaction to the fact that his former Marine instructor was dismissed from the service for being gay. In saying the man was one of the best soldiers he knew, and had once saved his life, he fastened instinctively on the genuine ground for discrimination, that of fitness to do the job. That the man passed that test with flying colours was all Paddy needed to know. He will be a hard act for another leader to follow, but if we leave out the training in unarmed combat, which is not in the routine leader's manual, I am sure he or she will succeed. A tradition of centuries is a powerful reinforcement.

4

The Underdog and the Economy

Robert Skidelsky, in his biography of Keynes, remarked that Victorian governments did not have an economic policy.[1] This remark may contain a pardonable element of hyperbole, yet it also expresses a truth. *A fortiori*, seventeenth- and eighteenth-century governments did not have anything we would now understand as an economic policy. This was not because they believed in any doctrine of non-intervention. They had to the full the desire of all government to have its own way, and where they could intervene, they did so with gusto.

What they lacked was control over the levers of economic power, or indeed any understanding of what those levers were. Dealing with economic crises tended to be a little like dealing with floods – a problem of mopping up the mess created by a deluge which could not be prevented.

It is perhaps because Liberal philosophy goes back into this period that the party does not have an economic philosophy. It has brought to economics a mixture of pragmatism and a series of philosophical convictions such as attachment to equal competition and support for the underdog, whose origins in party thinking lie well outside economics. It is the standard mistake of the twentieth century in studying the nineteenth to assume that divisions were rooted in economics which in fact were rooted in religion. The history of the Liberal Party is perhaps one of the fields which have suffered most severely from this tendency. Karl Marx, in a well-known phrase, said that Liberalism 'gave effect to the sway of free competition within the realm of knowledge'.[2] This remark needs to be treated the way Marx treated Hegel: it needs to be stood right side up. Read that way, it might be more accurately expressed in the words: 'Liberalism gave effect to the doctrine of religious pluralism within the realm of the economy.' The doctrine of religious pluralism, for historical reasons, always married in Liberal minds a gut commitment to equal competition with a gut commitment to support the underdog. This was the mentality Liberals brought into the task of acquiring an economic policy.

This lack of an economic philosophy has been both a strength and a weakness to the party. It has been a strength in that it has created an adaptability which has made it possible for the party to produce policies suiting each stage of economic thinking in turn, without needing to be false to any of its basic beliefs. It is a party which has been able to produce policies for the age of Mill's *Principles of Political Economy*, and for the age of Keynes's *General Theory*. Nothing in changing economic circumstances is likely to spell disaster for Liberals the way it spelt disaster for Labour in 1976 when Jim Callaghan had to explain that it was no longer possible to spend one's way out of a recession, or the way it does for the Conservatives as they begin to face the central fact of globalisation, that the nation state and the free market are no longer compatible. It gives the party great adaptability. It enables it to face up to expert opinion.

Yet there is also weakness in this pragmatism. It may make us too easy victims for the latest fashionable economist to capture the headlines, and may make us go too far in embracing the philosophy of the moment. Both in the fashionable addiction to *laissez-faire* of the 1840s, and in the ultra-Keynesian demand management of the incomes policies of the 1970s, we probably made significant mistakes by conforming to the prevailing philosophy of the moment. A clearer economic philosophy of our own might have acted as a sheet-anchor to hold us back from this too easy following of fashion.

Perhaps it is more serious that the lack of a clear commitment leaves opponents free to impose a cartoon image of their own choosing. Anyone who remembers the cartoonists' treatment of John Major will see how serious this danger can become. If Liberal economic policy has fallen victim to cartoons devised in the interests of our opponents, we have in part ourselves to blame.

Perhaps the most successful of these, recently repeated by Tony Blair, is the attempt to portray us as in essence a party of *laissez-faire*. For a while, especially in the 1840s, *laissez-faire* was a fashionable creed, encouraged by the works of the classical economists, and therefore one held in some quarters within the party. Yet even then, it was never a simple majority creed of the party, nor even a peculiar creed of Liberals or Whigs. Probably the most purely *laissez-faire* administration of the nineteenth century was Peel's, and Peel was certainly not a Liberal. Even in the 1840s, Whigs or Liberals aroused vigorous attacks from believers in *laissez-faire* who complained they did not understand the creed. In 1847, the *Leeds Mercury* denounced those who 'yield to the pertinacity of those who demand legislative interference with the ordinary and natural course of manufacturing industry'.[3] This was an attack on a Whig government led by Russell, which had used its power to secure the passage of the Ten Hours Bill, limiting hours of work. It was Peel who had upheld his commitment to *laissez-faire* economics by refusing to accept the Bill, even when offered a substantial compromise.

As the nineteenth century went on, the party moved farther and farther away from this fashion, until the New Liberalism of the 1906 government supported a degree of intervention which laid the foundations of the modern Welfare State. None of this has stopped the endless succession of attacks on Liberals as a *laissez-faire* party. Michael Freeden, the historian of New Liberalism, complained that 'modern Liberalism has suffered mainly through sheer ignorance of its nature. Even now, many of its modern opponents assail with venom a set of principles that Liberalism itself discarded almost a century ago.' That is an academic, not a political, judgement. He also remarked that 'by the end of the 1880s, the *laissez-faire* credo was more likely to be heard from Conservatives of the type of Lord Wemyss'.[4] When George Goschen complained of the party's lack of commitment to 'political economy', he deserves attention because this was the reason he was giving for leaving the party. Sidney Webb, a critic from the other side, said: 'The Liberal Party is in no way pledged, if indeed it ever was, to a blind allegiance to *laissez-faire*.' In 1959, Jo Grimond, perhaps more committed to restricting the role of government than any other leader since the war, said the Liberals never were a party of pure *laissez-faire*.[5] Eugenio Biagini, wearing an academic hat, has perhaps gone farther than any of them. He has written: 'In contrast with the old Thatcherite or "Newt Gingrichite" stereo-typical image of "Victorian values" – meaning individualism, self-help and *laissez-faire* – and the endorsement of similar myths by some Socialist historians, we elaborate on the thesis that politics in the nineteenth and early twentieth centuries was not primarily about the individual's rights, but about the repre-sentation of his community.'[6] I can recall Lord Beveridge, speaking in the Oxford Union at the protest meeting against Suez in 1956, saying something very similar about the twentieth century's mis-understanding of 'Victorian values'. A consensus so powerful deserves at least a hearing.

Views on economic questions were not what held the party together. In Jonathan Parry's words, 'most whigs attached more importance to political structures than to economic laws'.[7] In spite of all his work on *The Principles of Political Economy*, this was also true of John Stuart Mill. Modern champions of the free market tend to regard Mill's *Essay on Liberty* and his *Principles of Political Economy* as expressions of a single united body of doc-trine, as defences of a 'liberty' which is economic, moral and political all in the same breath. It is interesting and perhaps remarkable that Mill, in Chapter 5 of his *Essay on Liberty*, went right out of his way to reject this interpretation of what he had done. This passage is worth repeating in full, since it shows with such clarity the philosophical gulf which divides John Stuart Mill from Milton Friedman, the moralist Free Marketeer from the pragmatist Free Trader. Mill was explaining that the principle stated in his *Essay on Liberty* had no application to the economy.

> Trade is a social act. Whoever undertakes to sell any descrip-tion of goods to the public, does what affects the interest of other persons, and of society in general; and thus his conduct, in principle, comes within the jurisdiction of society: accord-ingly, it was once held to be the duty of governments, in all cases which were considered of importance, to fix prices, and regulate the processes of manufacture. But it is now recog-

nised, though not till after a long struggle, that both the cheapness and the good quality of commodities are most effectually provided for by leaving the producers and sellers perfectly free, under the sole check of equal freedom for the buyers for supplying themselves elsewhere. This is the so-called doctrine of Free Trade, which rests on grounds different from, though equally solid with, the principle of individual liberty asserted in this essay.[8]

This is Liberal free trade thinking at its height, and it stops far short of the extravagances of modern free market theory. Mill, like Peter Lilley today, could see a big difference between the functioning of a market and the discharge of a public service, and did not think that the principles of one necessarily had to be applied to the other. In this, he had the agreement of all Victorians of almost any political persuasion whatsoever. He recognised, in the passage immediately following this one, the case for state intervention to prevent adulteration or fraud, for sanitary purposes, or to preserve health and safety at work. He thought the burden of proof should rest on the state in such intervention, since other things being equal liberty was preferable to control, but he did not see such intervention as a burden on business or a distortion of the market. It was part of the state's duty of protection.

Today, when we tend to think of the free market as a place where the sharks eat up the minnows, it is a shock to realise that Victorian Liberals regarded Free Trade as largely a device for the protection of the poor against the rich. Without this, the continuity of the party from Mill and Gladstone to Lloyd George, Keynes and Beveridge would not have been possible.

Liberal thought has always included a practical egalitarianism which owes more to the *Magnificat* than to Marx: 'He hath put down the mighty from their seats, and exalted them of low degree. He hath filled the hungry with good things, and the rich he hath sent empty away.' John Wilson, Methodist preacher and Durham Miners' leader, recalling the 1840s, talked of the days when government 'taxed the coal to save the landlords' pockets – taxed the sugar to save the pockets that might bear the taxation – put a corn tax on, and it was a burden to the widow and orphan to save the rich. They had filled the rich with good things, and the poor they had sent empty away.'[9] We can hear the angry inversion of the *Magnificat* in the condemnation.

The cry of Free Trade, especially in the context of the issue of the Corn Laws where the party developed it, was essentially a cry for cheap food. That was a popular cry. 'The great, practical, easily-understood Anti-Corn Law League, which had the cheap loaf on its banner, drowned the clamour of Chartism. ... The Big Loaf had the better of the Big Talk.'[10] The slogan of the Free Traders was the Free Breakfast Table – the items on it all un-taxed, and the tax falling on landowners who could well afford to pay it. As late as the 1906 election, when Chamberlain tried to revive Protection, Lloyd George dismissed it in the devastatingly populist cry of 'stomach taxes'.

It is striking to a modern ear that Millicent Garrett Fawcett, in her essay on *Why I Am A Liberal*, condemned legislative attacks on Trade Unions as an interference with the free market. This is a world in some ways unfamiliar to post-Thatcherite ears, and ideas should not be translated from one to the other without a dictionary. One clue comes from the regular hostility to the Game Laws, which were described as 'a badge of serfdom and slavery for farmer and peasant'.[11]

The clue is the extent to which the radical cutting edge of Free Trade ideology in the 1840s was aimed at land, and land was seen as a natural monopoly. There is much truth in this analysis: as Ruth Coleman said at our party conference in 1999, 'Trouble is, they're not making land any more'.[12] Because land was a natural monopoly, competition with cheap foreign corn was the only way its monopoly power could be controlled, and the only way the power of the rich to oppress the poor could be limited. It was Mill, no less, who denounced landlords because they 'grow rich in their sleep, without working, risking or economising'.[13] A modern free market believer would not understand what was bothering Mill. This was the ground on which a radical reforming party took up the ideology of free trade, and on which monopoly came to the top of the Liberal demonology. In the words of the *Leicester Daily Mercury* in 1909, Liberals were against 'monopolies in land, in liquor, ecclesiasticism, in electoral machinery, and in the House of

Lords, which is the very holy of holies of monopoly'.[14] There is a very clear continuity here, stretching from the attacks on the monopoly of the Church of England down to the attempts, in 1998, to control the monopoly power of Rupert Murdoch by amendments to tighten the Competition Bill. The purpose of competition was to storm the economic castles of monopolists who had protected themselves against it. Once this thrust of support for the underdog is understood, changes in Liberal economic policy may seem less dramatic than pure economic thought would take them to be.

With this horror of monopoly came the regular Liberal desire to control the abuse of power. That desire had never been confined to the power of the state. In the Llanfrothen burial case, for example, for example, it was the arbitrary power of the Rector to lock the gates of his churchyard which caused the crisis, and the power of the state, acting through a recent Act of Parliament, which left the oppressed widow free to bury her husband. Liberal struggles with the church had taught them from the beginning that the state could be a liberator as well as an oppressor. That is a lesson which, even in the heyday of *laissez-faire*, has never been forgotten, and has now come back into the heart of the party's thinking about liberty.

It is instructive to look at the limits to free enterprise which were accepted in the party's most free market days, because many of them are ground we are defending against Thatcherite notions of free enterprise at the moment. The first category of exceptions was the natural monopolies, such as railways, which Gladstone, and even so respectable a Whig as Hartington, were prepared to contemplate taking into public ownership.[15] With them came such unpromising areas for competition as the sewers and the electric telegraph. Ebrington, one of the key supporters of Russell and Carlisle's Public Health Act of 1848, argued for sanitary legislation because the remedies were 'beyond the reach of individuals'. It is no use complaining that public services inhibit freedom of choice if the choices, such as that of building sewers, are beyond the power of individuals to make. This point has as much force, and is as often needed in debate, today as it was in 1848. So is Ebrington's further point that 'all that impaired the health of the working class entailed positive loss upon the community'.[16] As it happened, chance rammed Ebrington's point home. The Public Health Act was in its first year of operation, and the Treasury was closing in for the kill, when the cholera struck, and Russell was able to order the Treasury not to undermine the Public Health Board, for it was acting for the public good. The cholera did more than Socialism ever did to expose the limits of *laissez-faire*.

The case for free competition must always depend on the claim that it is fair competition. The satirical description 'freedom for ever, said the elephant, as he trampled among the chickens', has never been Liberal policy. There has always been a reservation that free competition must be competition between those able to compete on equal terms. This rules out monopoly, and it rules out cases where the inequality of power is so gross that any notion of free competition is a mockery. It is the doctrine now known as the doctrine of the level playing field. This is one the party has adhered to for as long as it has had any economic policy, and it still does. As L.T. Hobhouse said, 'Liberty without equality is a name of noble sound and squalid result'. He said freedom of contract was not freedom at all if one side was constrained by poverty or otherwise impeded from rational prosecution of its interests. On another occasion, Hobhouse defended legislation against monopolies on the ground that it was 'directed to the redressing of inequality in bargaining ... not an infringement of the two distinctive ideas of the older liberalism, "liberty and equality", but rather a necessary means to their fulfilment'.[17]

Hobhouse was one of the prophets of New Liberalism, on which Asquith and Lloyd George drew so heavily when they set up Wages Councils, Old Age Pensions and National Insurance. There is a temptation to see Hobhouse as representing the way in which New Liberalism differed from the Liberalism of earlier generations. Yet Hobhouse was explicitly claiming a continuity. Does this claim stand up? This is more an argument about differences of emphasis than about qualitiative change. It is certainly a note heard oftener in the New Liberal era before the First World War, and certainly one pressed much further than it had been before. Yet the basic principles are ones which had been there long before. They are clearly set out, for example, by Harcourt in 1880, introducing what became the Ground Game Act. This Act allowed tenants to shoot rabbits which ate their crops, whatever objection landlords might make to the threat to their game rights. It righted a long-standing tenant grievance, but it offended Conservative landlords on the ground that it interfered with their freedom of contract. Harcourt replied that freedom of contract was a very valuable principle, but 'all principles, however sound they might be, were subject to clear and well-defined exceptions'. 'Where bad customs had grown up, and one party had been unable to resist the force of those bad customs, then Parliament had stepped in and broken through the customs and forbidden them. On that principle it was that Parliament had interfered with the Truck Acts between the employer and employed, and forbidden the payment of wages in food or other commodities, and had declared that any contract with wages, other than in coin, should be illegal, null and void. That was an interference with freedom of contract.'[18] Harcourt gave a long list of further examples, and they were soundly chosen.

This readiness to intervene to redress the effects of a gross inequality of power was behind all the exceptions to market freedom which the party had allowed in its most *laissez-faire* days. Even Mill allowed exceptions for education, poor relief, hospitals and other public services, limitations of hours of labour, and regulation of conditions of work. Many restrictions, especially on such things as child labour, were accepted on moral rather than market grounds.

The lack of equality of power was used to justify regulation of health and safety at work. An article in *Reynolds's News* in 1875, asked 'is a man free to commit suicide? If not, he is hardly free to go down into a coal pit. Talk of freedom indeed! Why, if a man brought up as a collier refuses to go down a pit which he knows to be fiery, he starves on the ground that he will not work, and if he works he is suffocated or burnt.'[19] He asked a series of similar questions about the safety of iron puddlers and sailors, and in each case gave his answers a double justification, out of the Bible and out of Mill's *Principles of Political Economy*.

Even in its most free market phase, the party was a dedicated defender of public services. It was always understood that there was a sphere for the market, and a sphere for public services. The fact that these two operations had different functions, different spheres and different purposes was no reason for denigrating either. There were three common reasons for defending a public service way of tackling a problem. The first was where, as in water and gas, the only alternatives were a private monopoly or total anarchy. It was not in the nature of the job to be done otherwise than as a public service. The second, used by Ebrington to justify public provision of sewers, was that remedies were 'beyond the reach of individuals'. Individuals could not choose to go into the market and buy a sewer. The job had to be done collectively or not at all.

The third was where the need was for the creation of an opportunity, which people could choose to put to use if they saw fit. The Public Libraries which were one of the glories of the nineteenth century were a typical example of this approach. So were the public baths so essential in Victorian towns. The crowning example was always education. Richard Cobden, not the greatest enemy of market provision in the Party, recommended 'a system of schools free to all, paid by all', to give 'everyone the opportunity to attend gratis'. In modern jargon, they were to be free at the point of delivery.[20] John Stuart Mill wanted the state to require everyone who had children to get them educated, and to provide money for those who could not otherwise afford it.[21] This was delivered by Forster's Education Act of 1870.

This use of the power of the State to create opportunity followed from Liberal definitions of liberty. Professor Biagini is right that the party never agreed with Hobbes that 'liberty is the absence of restraint'. That purely negative definition of liberty leads to Thatcherism, not to Liberalism. It leads to an identification of liberty with minimum government action, and that is something in which Liberals have never believed. That is the liberty of the powerful: it is not the liberty of a party which, at all stages of its existence, has been dedicated to defending the powerless against privilege.

For John Stuart Mill, speaking without thinking and therefore saying what he thought, 'liberty consists in doing what one desires'.[22] This is very much more Isaiah Berlin's notion of 'positive liberty', 'freedom to', rather than 'freedom from'. It was in fact this positive liberty for which the party had been fighting right back to the very beginning of the attempt to secure equal rights for Dissenters. Freedom to be buried in consecrated ground, freedom to hold public office without taking the Sacrament in the Church of England, freedom to enter Oxford and Cambridge, or freedom to sit in Parliament without taking the oath – these were all positive liberties. They were opportunities to exercise choices, to be won by legislative action and defended by the State against the intolerance of those who would deny them. That history alone would have been enough to preserve the party from being the totally free market party of Thatcherite caricature. Its whole history had taught it to see liberty as opportunity to be won by state action. It had taught it that oppression could be the work of other powerful bodies, such as the established church, as well as of the state. It had taught it to see liberty, not as minimum government, but as minimum oppression.

It has struck me very forcibly, while doing the reading which has gone into this chapter, that almost every argument I find that the party has used to put limits to *laissez-faire* in the middle of the nineteenth century is one which I have myself used during the 1980s and 1990s against the extension of the Thatcherite Market of Hope and Glory, claiming that wider still and wider shall its bounds be set. The arguments against a private monopoly, used to justify public provision of sewage and water, are the same I used against the Water Bill in 1989. The argument that it is beyond the reach of individuals is the same I have used for provision of more public transport. The arguments of inequality of power are the same I have used for the minimum wage, or for the Working Hours Directive. The arguments for the duty of the state to create opportunities are the same I have used against cutbacks in funding for students. We want the best, not the richest. It is what my great-grandfather would have called the *'carrière ouverte au talent'*. When I picked these arguments, often spontaneously in debate, I did not know that I was following what the party had said 150 years before. This spontaneous reaching for the same arguments, and even more the constant finding of arguments a hundred years old and more which I could recycle in Parliament tomorrow, do appear to me to be evidence of a continuing party philosophy, which is as alive, and as fresh, today, as any time in the party's history.

It has, of course, varied enormously in line with prevailing economic theory and prevailing economic circumstance. The economic policy of the middle of the nineteenth century was designed for a world in which full employment was instinctively assumed to be the economic norm. That assumption was recognised as becoming threadbare before the beginning of the 1906 government, and that realisation contributed a great deal to the 1906 government's increasingly activist approach to economic and social policy. Those assumptions which had underpinned nineteenth-century policy were buried in Keynes's 1924 Lecture on *The End of Laissez-Faire*. They have never come back.

The advent of the global market, and of the multinational company, have greatly increased the potential inequality of power between employer and employee. To that, too, the party has reacted, in being willing to extend far more protection to victims of economic power than it ever contemplated in the nineteenth century. This change, too, is unlikely ever to go into reverse. The dedication to minimum oppression, rather than to minimum government, is in the party's bedrock. Such unequal exercises of power as that of the employer who dismissed a pregnant employee on the ground that it was 'unnatural' will always hit the Liberal conscience between wind and water. These things are unlikely to change.

Keynes's personal economic theories are in some points another matter. Since the collapse of the international monetary agreement reached by Keynes at Bretton Woods in 1945, and since the collapse of his theories of demand management, we can probably not again hope to fight an election on quite so interventionist an approach to unemployment as Keynes and Lloyd George attempted in 1929. On the other hand, though Keynes's theories about demand management may not stand, his theories about the risks of inadequate demand to the world economy emphatically do stand.

Since the collapse of Bretton Woods in 1971, and even more since the abolition of exchange controls in 1979, we have been moving into a new economic world. The total freedom of capital movement around the world, compared with the much restricted freedom of movement of labour, has created a world playing field which is very far from level. The ability of industry to move manufacture from country to country in search of the lowest cost threatens a cost-cutting war of great intensity. Unwarily undertaken, this could lower world demand to a level where the global economy is seriously at risk from slump. It almost happened in 1998, and the risk will recur.

It is easy enough, using the material already in this chapter, to sketch the philosophical outline of a Liberal response to this development. Extreme inequalities of power, lack of a level playing field, and monopoly power of oppression are all things to which there are standard Liberal reflexes. Yet none of these are things the nation state can now tackle. New policies are needed. How far this can be done is a question for the last chapter.

5

Internationalism

If the commitment to the underdog which underpins the party's economic policy is largely a legacy of the early and middle nineteenth century, the internationalism which underpins its foreign policy is largely the legacy of Gladstone. At the time, much of Gladstone's internationalism passed the rank and file of the party by. Bulgaria, like Kosovo, did not necessarily play well on the doorsteps. The influence of Bulgaria, and probably of Kosovo too, is important for what it contributed to the Liberal legacy. It had a defining importance in what it meant to later generations to be a Liberal, which it did not have in the Midlothian election of 1880.

There are two issues with which Gladstone forced the party to grapple, which have been with us ever since. One is the issue of the nation state and how the party should view it. This is something on which party thinking appears to have changed fundamentally since Gladstone's time, yet it can perhaps be argued that there is an underlying consistency holding these apparently different views together. Nancy Seear, my former Deputy Leader in the Lords, once hissed into my ear during a boring committee meeting: '*Why* were we so much for the nation state in the nineteenth century, and so much against it now?' I replied on the spur of the moment: 'I'm not sure, but I think it's something to do with consent.' This chapter is designed, in part, to take that answer further.

The other thing we owe to Gladstone is the internationalisation of our commitment to the underdog. This has produced a much straighter line of development to a firm legal commitment to international human rights. In this internationalisation of our concern with rights, Gladstone's Christianity played a very large part. Gladstone, unusually for a Liberal leader, was not merely an Anglican, which many others had been, but a High Churchman as well. What made him into a Liberal, after beginning his career as 'the rising hope of the stern unbending Tories', was his increasing commitment to a degree of separation of church and state, in order to protect the church from the intervention of low church governments. It is this commitment to a particular wing of the Church of England which gave him that pluralism which made him a sort of political equivalent of a Dissenter when the right of variety was in question. At all times when human rights were in question, Gladstone's commitment was the Christian one to the underlying equality of every human soul. One soul in Afghanistan had the same rights as one soul in Aberdeen, and one soul in Bulgaria had the same rights as one soul in Birmingham.

What the party has done with this commitment since is to apply its instinctive identification of liberty with law, and tie it into the rapidly developing framework of international law. Since the Nuremberg trials, and since the foundation of the United Nations in 1945, the development of international law has been dominated by a series of conventions drawn up under the auspices of the UN. The UN Convention Against Torture, which determined the result of General Pinochet's extradition hearing, is only one among many of these. International lawyers now tend to treat these conventions, especially if incorporated in domestic law, as a sort of international legislation, which can be applied in judgements of courts. This trend is still gathering momentum, and at the time of the Pinochet trial, it had only just gone far enough to carry the judgement. Many politicians have been surprised to discover quite how far it had gone. Liberals and Liberal Democrats have tended to be in the forefront of understanding and applying it. It expresses Gladstone's commitment to international human rights in a framework which is legal and secular, and therefore suits the party extremely well. In the process, however, it has helped to lead the party far away from Gladstone's other belief in the sovereign nation state.

Though Gladstone is rightly identified with the rise of the commitment to the nation state, it in fact begins with Liberal welcomes for the movement for Italian Unification, and the key moment is perhaps Russell's dispatch to the British minister in Turin in October 1860. It makes the point about continuity that Russell's commitment was made because he recognised a continuity between what the Italians were doing and what the Whigs had done in 1688. At one tense moment, the Queen asked him: 'Am I to understand you to say, Lord John, that under certain circumstances subjects may resist their lawful sovereign?' He replied: 'Speaking to a sovereign of the House of Hanover, Ma'am, I think I may say that I do.'[1] The key principle was that of government by consent. That was something which Austrian rule in Italy could not claim, and nationalism was seen as expressing a view that nations should be governed by their own consent. That is why Russell's dispatch invoked 1688, and talked of 'a people building up the edifice of their liberties'.[2]

Gladstone, at first was rather less sure of touch on the issue of nationalism and consent. He understood the point Thatcherites have been so unable to grasp, that nations are not God-given entities, but human creations which are the result of changes in human feeling. Where he was less certain, before his commitment to franchise reform, was on the question whose consent was required for the creation of a nation. That appears to be the explanation of his Newcastle speech of 1862, which said that 'there is no doubt that Jefferson Davis and other leaders of the (American) South have made an army; they are making, it appears, a navy; and they have made what is more difficult than either, they have made a nation'. He was not the last Liberal to make this mistake. The independence of South Africa, granted by the Asquith government, is the only time Britain has handed over power in a former colony to a minority. It is an old-fashioned relic of eighteenth-century thinking to regard 'the people' as anything less than the total body of adults living there. At least by 1896, with his views on the franchise developed by two further Reform Bills, Gladstone understood he had done wrong. He described it as 'only a mistake, but one of incredible grossness'.[3] In the 1880s, when he talked of the Moslems of the Sudan as 'a people rightly struggling to be free',[4] he does seem to have meant all the people. In Ireland, his commitment to national Home Rule followed imme-

diately on the Third Reform Bill, which had at least given the vote
to a high proportion of adult Irish males. However, the Irish case
does at least illustrate one big difference between Gladstonian
nationalism and Thatcherite national sovereignty. Gladstone did
not think that the recognition of Ireland as a nation to be governed
by its own consent necessarily implied its recognition as a sovereign state. He thought it quite compatible with its continuation in
a pluralist union with England and Scotland. His parallel was not
taken from a modern nation state, but from a traditional dynastic
one. It was the union of Austria and Hungary while each retained
its separate legislature.

Ireland also exposed the paradoxes and weaknesses of Gladstonian nationalism. Professor Biagini is surely right that Ulster
is the place where 'Midlothian Liberalism' was undermined by its
own logic. Gladstone, as his Newcastle speech on the American
South illustrated, did not believe in immutable and natural 'nations'. He believed nations were man-made. He did not accept the
Irish Nationalist view that Ireland is a Platonic entity of 32
counties, and only the assent of all 32 counties can ever bind it. So
if Ireland could withdraw from rule by England because it did not
consent to it, why could not Ulster withdraw from rule by Ireland
because it did not consent to it? Was it not a case of 'great nations
have little nations upon their backs to bite 'em', to paraphrase the
famous jingle? This view of nationalism was parodied in 1917 by a
single house which barricaded itself against the Bolsheviks, and
sent a telegram to Woodrow Wilson claiming that it was a nation
rightly struggling to be free – a phrase, incidentally, which, it
seems, Gladstone never used.

After the great nation-creating celebration of Versailles, the
slow breaking up of Woodrow Wilson's nations, of which the case
of Yugoslavia may serve for a caricature, rapidly undermined the
traditional Liberal identification of nationalism with government
by consent. There are many cases, of which Bosnia and Northern
Ireland are two of the most obvious, where any requirement that
a state must require a single 'nation' to inhabit it either leads to
ethnic cleansing, or must make all government impossible. The
world is simply not sorted into ethnically defined 'nations'. In some
cases, such as Poland, a state may be based on national consent,

but even there, there are racial minorities to whom rights of citizenship must be extended. If consent cannot be made independent of race, government by consent in many parts of the globe is totally impossible.

One commentator has remarked that 'British Liberals could admire ... nationalism without appreciating the ways in which its central features ran contrary to their own state interests'.[5] Because the nationalism of British Liberals was based on a multinational state and on the separation of church and state, they always had a pluralist conception of a nation, in which common consent in citizenship inside a nation was compatible with racial and intellectual plurality inside it. It was the nationalism of Fluellen and Macmorris in Shakespeare's *Henry V*, in which unity was cemented by the sparring over the difference. It was a very Parliamentary concept of nationality.

It therefore took Liberals some time to realise quite how restrictive, and repressive, pure ethnic nationalism was capable of being. This was the truer for the fact that Mazzini, together with Kossuth, the first European nationalists who became popular heroes in England, was very recognisably a Liberal. His was a very civilised nationalism.

The encounter with the raw irredentist nationalism of Greater Serbia, at Sarajevo in 1914, was rapidly overlaid by so many other things that the impact was less great than it might otherwise have been. It was not, perhaps, until the encounter with the death-dealing nationalism of Hitler that it was widely clear to Liberals quite what a dangerous beast nationalism was capable of being. Nancy Seear, who was in Germany in 1932, recollected many years later that 'the angel of death was abroad in the land'.

This doubt about nationalism as the basis of consent was strengthened by growing awareness of all those places where ethnic identity did not coincide with frontiers. Before the war, the Sudeten Germans were one of the most obvious examples. Africa, where tribal divisions were very far from coinciding with the places where the Great Powers had drawn lines on the map, was another very obvious case. The attempt of Nehru and Gandhi to stand out in India for a British Liberal concept of secular nationalism against the communalist nationalisms of Hindu and Moslem was a magnificent attempt, but its birth in 1947 was greeted with massive rioting in the name of a narrow communal nationalism which stood for everything Liberals did not believe. It is perhaps because India sees yielding over Kashmir as a surrender to the communal pattern of nationalism that its resistance to any change in the status of Kashmir has been so adamant. Yet when this conflicts with the principle of self-determination, the basic application of the Liberal principle of government by consent, Liberals are impaled on the horns of a dilemma. Cases like these have taught Liberals that nationalism can be the enemy of government by consent as well as its friend.

When this happened, consent, which was the essence of Liberal philosophy of government, was always going to take priority over nationalism, which was merely one of its accidents. Here, as in so many other places, we are looking at a consistent Liberal principle which, in different circumstances, has been expressed in apparently contradictory ways. From the outside, the difference looks obvious. From the inside, the consistency looks obvious. Both perspectives are valid in their own right, but if we are describing how a party looks to itself, it is the internal perspective which is relevant to our immediate question.

Faced with a diminishing affection for nationalism, we have developed the other part of Gladstone's legacy, which is the commitment to international human rights. In his description of the chaining of prisoners in Naples as 'the negation of God erected into a system of government', or in his declaration that human life in the hill villages of Afghanistan 'is as inviolable in the eyes of Almighty God as can be your own', Gladstone did not only anchor Liberal commitment to human rights in Christian belief. He also anchored it in the original Liberal belief that, logically and chronologically, people are before government.

This now shows up, first and foremost, in the gut Liberal commitment to defend the rights of refugees seeking asylum. If they cannot live at peace in their own countries, then it is part of their human rights that they should be able to live at peace somewhere else. We are very aware, as a party, how much the country has benefited from past waves of refugees. The thought of countries competing with each other to see who can deter refugees

most effectively revolts us. It is to foreign affairs what child labour
is to the economy: a cut-throat competition which lowers all who
take part in it, to the detriment of the world in which we must all
live. The festering resentment inside Palestinian refugee camps,
and the occasional acts of terrorism in which it finds expression,
are painful reminders that self-interest here goes along with idealism. A world regulated by some international order is a much
more Liberal world than one in which unregulated competition
enables the strong to oppress the weak to the best of their ability.

We are also well aware of the limits of the nation state as a
means of tackling international problems. Even if it is sheer
military might alone which is needed, some form of international
co-operation is always going to be needed. Even if it were not, the
idea of one great power being able to act as the world's policeman
has considerable disadvantages, as Nicaragua and Grenada have
learnt. As a party, we began to learn this through our own experience in the last century. Moves towards collective security,
through the League of Nations and then the United Nations,
have built on many instinctive Liberal reflexes towards order
and consent.

Unfortunately, the present constitution of the UN, and the facts
of world power to which that constitution gives expression, do not
allow collective security enough authority. The UN's one really
conspicuous success in turning back aggression, in Korea, de-
pended on the accident of a Russian walkout, which has not been
repeated. Because the world's military force remains, for the present, in the hands of a limited number of great powers, a military
operation which one of them opposes is extremely hard to conduct.
The attempt, in Kosovo, to use international Human Rights law to
bypass the UN ran into great dangers, as was shown by the sudden
appearance of the Russians at Pristina airport. This is not to say
that the dangers were greater than those of inaction. The reverse
is probably the case. It is to say that the present situation is very
far from satisfactory. The attempt to restrict armed action to the
UN probably cannot be effective unless the UN should have something like the European Union's qualified majority voting instead
of the veto. If that were the case, it would mean that the balance
of power in the world had already become other than it is.

The UN is also hamstrung in many situations by its commitment to national sovereignty. Article 2 of the UN Charter forbids
interference in the internal affairs of a member state. At first
sight, this seems fair enough. We do not want to go back to a
nineteenth-century world in which, in the memorable parody of
1066 And All That, the British government could intervene in
Afghanistan to make the Emir 'sit on his throne in a more friendly
attitude'. In so far as that is the effect of Article 2, it is a good one.

Yet it is not that simple either. The concept of an 'internal affair'
has an inherent ambiguity. To say that an issue is one properly
legally determined according to the principles of national sovereignty is not to say that it is incapable of being a threat to
international peace and security. To take one elementary example,
what happened to the nuclear reactor at Chernobyl has led to
nuclear pollution, and possibly to loss of life, as far away as
Sweden and North Wales. To call the neglect of the Chernobyl
reactor an 'internal affair' is straining language.

I recall watching the television pictures in 1990 of Iraqui Kurds
struggling and stumbling over the mountains to arrive destitute
in Turkey (hardly the safest of havens for Kurds) because Saddam
Hussein had made them too afraid to stay. A million Kurds took
part in that exodus, and they created a massive relief problem. It
hit me in that moment that the act of sending a million people
destitute into the territory of another country cannot easily be
regarded as an 'internal affair', even if it is true that the doctrine
of national sovereignty places no restriction on the right of a
government to persecute its own subjects. Gladstone's phrase
about King Bomba of Naples, 'the negation of God erected into a
system of government' comes back to mind. Because we are human, and because we have to clear up the mess, it is our business.
As usual, principle and self-interest go hand in hand. Watching
refugees from Slobodan Milosevic held on the border of Macedonia
at Blace, and listening to the eloquent dismay of the Macedonian
government about what the Serbs had done to Macedonia, I learnt
these lessons all over again. Other Liberals have learnt them in
other places, but in one way or another, the lesson has been widely
learnt around the party. The result has been a vigorous debate, in
which David Steel has been in the lead, about the case for amend-

ing Article 2 of the UN Charter. The reflexes behind this go back to Locke's idea of the Law of Nature, as well as drawing on the practical facts of power in the modern world. Yet the issue is not simple. I recall, in the foreign affairs debate at our Harrogate Conference in 1992, David Steel had led the party along the road of supporting revision. His case was just about to be supported by a stampede when Eduardo Reyes, one of the ablest of the younger members, asked whether anyone would contemplate applying this doctrine against the domestic policy of the United States if it should cause sufficient outrage. He impaled the party on a fork. If they said 'yes', they committed themselves to something they could not enforce. If they said 'no', they gave up any pretence at that equality in the face of power at which all Liberals must aim. I see no way off his fork.[6]

Behind all this lies a steadily growing Liberal doubt whether the powers of a single sovereign state are capable even of addressing, let alone solving, the main problems of running a modern world. The abuses of power which give rise to conflicts, and the scarcity of resources which give rise to conflicts, neither of them are capable of being addressed by state power. The big concentrations of economic power tend to be in multinational companies, and while one need not necessarily accept the demonology sometimes applied to multinational companies, there should be a healthy tension between economic power and political power. Neither should enjoy the monopoly power to have things all their own way. This is not something the present relationship between economic and political power can deliver. Unaccountable power, on Actonian principles, should always be a matter of alarm, and our present system can do nothing to ease that alarm. Whether it is exploitation of child labour or serious international pollution, one nation state against a large multinational company simply lacks the power necessary to produce a sporting contest.

What is true of economic power is even truer of environmental power, especially since it is often unwittingly exercised. The possibility that Americans driving to work may put Pacific islands or East Anglian villages under water must be a real one, and it is hard to see how a merely national authority can have the power which might be necessary to stop this happening. With rising population, we seem to be moving at the same time into a period of widespread shortages of fresh water. Many of the world's great rivers, the Indus and the Euphrates, to mention only two, pass through many states, and extraction from their headwaters may threaten the livelihood of states lower down the river.

Even military power seems to be escaping from the control of sovereign states. Both the portable easily concealed bomb and the alarmingly free market in Kalashnikovs and such weapons have created the possibility of an alarming amount of military power which is not under state control. The IRA, to take only one example recently familiar to English readers, is a military force of some significance without in any way representing the authority of a state. Paddy Ashdown, speaking at Chatham House in March 1996, said that at the time of speaking, 79 out of 82 armed conflicts in progress were not wars between states, but conflicts between groups, either within a state, or on a cross-border basis. War used to be the mark of the sovereign state. The present military balance seems to be reverting to an early mediaeval pattern in which the state's aim to monopolise armed force appeared to be plainly utopian.

I can remember, as recently as the 1960s, believing that the trends were going exactly the other way, and that air power was conferring on the organised military force of major states a degree of power they had never had before. I had not then appreciated the force of Mao Tse-Tung's discovery that guerrillas could conceal themselves among a sympathetic civilian population. One cannot bomb West Belfast, Jaffna or Gaza into oblivion. This leaves the military might of major states looking like John Wayne trying to shoot a mosquito. Perhaps I am wrong now as I was in the 1960s. I would like to think so, but it would be unwise to gamble on it. We need a world in which international standards of behaviour can be agreed and enforced, and in which conflicts can be mediated or brokered. Our present state system cannot deliver this. As Paddy Ashdown said, 'the idea that the sovereign nation state can remain the basis on which the world is managed is one of the nostalgic myths from which we are going to have to break free'.[7]

There is nothing distinctively Liberal about this realisation. In academic circles, it is a commonplace. What we perhaps can claim is that as a party, we are culturally better placed to adapt to it, because we have never been obsessed with believing in a unitary centre of power. We have always believed in plural centres of power, and we have believed for a long time that human rights and other issues create norms of international conduct whose authority goes well beyond any one sovereign state. It leaves us well equipped, in particular, to understand and welcome the rapid development of international law which is one of the bright spots on a largely gloomy horizon.

It is not too difficult, if one were in a utopian mood, to sketch out some of the very rough outlines of a Liberal international order. It would rest on consent, which would have to come in the first instance from sovereign states limiting their power in their own self-interest. It would rest on international law developed by a series of international convention under the auspices of the UN. Those on refugees, torture and genocide are all good and relevant models. This principle of binding international agreements, enforceable in courts, would be extended from Human rights to the environment, again with self-interest as the driving motive. Somewhere and somehow, there would need to be international military force capable of enforcing these international agreements. Here even the utopian's vision becomes cloudy, for it is not clear how this could be done.

Building utopias may be great fun, and it may serve to clear our minds about our ultimate objectives. Yet as soon as we take utopias seriously, building them ceases to be a Liberal activity. All utopias depend on one person's vision taking priority over another's and therefore they all come into existence, if at all, by the draconian enforcement of one person's vision on others. All utopias are potentially dictatorial. The beauty of the idealism is soon taken to obscure the beastliness of the enforcement. This is why utopias are not a Liberal pursuit. A creed which is founded on consent and on respect for difference of ideals is one which can dream dreams, but when awake, it can never be utopian without abandoning its own essence.

This is why we cannot aim straight for the utopia here sketched out. There is no alternative to consent. That takes the form of small piecemeal agreements, halfway acceptable operations such as that in Kosovo, which achieve some part of what was aimed at, and a general preference for a quarter of a loaf rather than no bread. Whether such methods will ever go fast enough to manage, for example, to stop global warming before we are under water, people may take leave to doubt. Yet however desperate the need for haste, there are no short cuts. Desperate need for haste does not make it possible to do a job faster than it can be done. The route by consent may be painfully slow, but it is the only route which does not become dictatorial and therefore self-defeating. It may not be fast enough to do what is needed, but it is the only route there is.

Liberty to Do What, May I Ask?

It is said that Jo Grimond, when he was leader of the Liberal
Party, was once asked how he managed to keep his Liberal faith
alive amid the press of petty business, and replied that he did it by
rereading Mill *On Liberty* once every year. This is something the
three Liberal Prime Ministers who had the chance to read the
Essay On Liberty in Mill's lifetime, Palmerston, Russell and Gladstone, would never have said. When Mill stood as Independent
Liberal candidate for Westminster, one Cabinet Minister was said
to have observed that the Almighty himself would not be elected
on such a programme – but Mill was.

Like Locke, Mill has been an acquired taste for his party. Both,
at the time when they wrote, were too far ahead of the game to get
that sort of reputation which is reserved for those who hit the
intellectual fashion of their own time. It is not merely in their own
countries, but in their own centuries, that prophets tend to lack
honour. Mill, though greatly esteemed, was regarded by politicians
as 'a bit extreme' when it came to his ideas on religion, morals and
liberty. In the Liberal Party, the book of office which was passed
on from the outgoing president to his successor was Milton's
Areopagitica. It was not until the foundation of the Liberal Democrats in 1988 that the Presidential book became Mill *On Liberty*.

That change marked an enlargement in the party's concept of
liberty which had already taken place, but which was confirmed
and strengthened by the merger with the SDP. Milton's *Areopagitica*, can still speak to a Liberal reader, but the political and
religious liberty of which Milton wrote is, except perhaps for
journalists and others facing overt or tacit censorship, no longer at

the cutting edge of debates on liberty. The liberty which is the flashpoint of debate now tends to be a more social and less political liberty, and concerns freedom in matters of morals rather than just in those of politics and religion. It is not that the old battles do not need refighting. They need it every day, as the issue of Freedom of Information is demonstrating at the moment. Yet these, though as vitally important as they ever were, are ones where the gambits are familiar. New ground may be opened up, as the issue of Freedom of Information illustrates, but the basic principles of openness and accountability are familiar. It is when we come to issues like whether marriage should be tax-neutral or the extent of homosexual equality that minds are being stretched and new ideas hammered out on the anvil of debate. These are among the issues where the unity of the Liberal and SDP wings of the party is most obvious, and these are the issues where Mill *On Liberty* is most clearly at the centre of debate. Some of the conclusions being drawn might have surprised Mill, but that is what, on his own principles, he should have expected.

Mill's key insight was that government by consent and accountability to a majority were not sufficient means of securing liberty. Mill, in 1859, was writing when the near approach of democracy was encouraging people to view it with an apprehensive eye. He was heavily influenced by de Tocqueville's *Democracy in America*, and by his own hostility to 'Mrs Grundy', the symbolic Jane Bull of Victorian respectability. He thought the tendency of society was 'to maim by compression, like a Chinese lady's foot, every part of human nature which stands out prominently'. He concluded that 'the people, consequently, *may* desire to oppress a part of their number'.[1]

It necessarily followed that the power of a majority, like that of any other government, must be controlled and subjected to limits. This was good traditional Liberal thinking, though its conclusions were unexpected to many Victorian Liberals. In his words: 'There is a limit to the legitimate interference of collective opinion with individual independence, and to find that limit, and maintain it against encroachment, is as indispensable to a good condition of human affairs, as protection against political despotism.'[2]

It is not often remarked how much, in attempting this task, Mill was following a trail the first part of which had been blazed by Locke in his *Letter Concerning Toleration*. Like Locke, Mill was proposing to restrict government interference by a new, and more limited, definition of the ends of government. Faced with anything not relevant to these ends, both replied that this was none of government's business. For Locke, enforcement of religion was none of government's business, and anything it attempted in that direction should be regarded as *ultra vires*. Mill took exactly the same arguments, with some additions, and attempted to extend them from religion to morals. In Locke's words 'the commonwealth seems to me to be a society of men constituted only for the procuring, preserving and advancing their own civil interests. Civil interest I call life, liberty, health and indolency of body; and the possession of outward things, such as money, lands, houses, furniture and the like. ... Now that the whole jurisdiction of the magistrate reaches only to these civil concernments; and that all civil power, right and dominion, is bounded and confined to the only care of promoting these things; and that it neither can nor ought to be extended to the salvation of souls, these following considerations seem to me abundantly to demonstrate. First, because the care of souls is not committed to the civil magistrate, any more than to other men. ... Nor can any such power be vested in the magistrate by consent of the people; because no man can so far abandon the care of his own salvation, as blindly to leave it to the choice of any other.'[3]

Mill's controversial contributions were to assert that the preservation of civil interests did not require a common system of morality, and, by applying the Christian and Liberal principle that one must follow one's conscience, to extend the principle of individual autonomy from the choice of faith to the choice of morals. That morals should be a matter of choice, as that religion should be a matter of choice, seemed to many to be a shocking abnegation of responsibility, and it is on this front that the great battles took place, and are continuing to take place.

Locke emphatically rejected any attempt to extend his doctrine of toleration from speculative theology to morals. In his words, 'a good life, in which consists not the least part of religion and true piety, concerns also the civil government, and in it lies the safety both of men's souls and of the commonwealth. Moral actions belong therefore to the jurisdiction both of the outward and the inward court; both of the civil and domestic governor; I mean, both of the magistrate and of the conscience.'[4]

It is important to understand how far both authors started from a desire to redefine the ends of government, since the fact goes some way to rebut the charge of religious and moral relativism which has been thrown against them ever since. It is true that both of them argued with force that none of us could have infallible certainty of the truth, and therefore all silencing of discussion was an assumption of infallibility. Yet every scholar, and every politician, can be certain of a belief without feeling the need to ban the contrary belief. Neither intended any prohibition on strongly held opinions: they had too many of their own. Their root position was that this was none of government's business, because it was not within its legitimate purposes.

This is how Mill arrived at his 'one very simple principle', 'that the only purpose for which power can be rightfully exercised over any member of a civilised community, against his will, is to prevent harm to others. His own good, either physical or moral, is not a sufficient warrant'.[5] From an academic point of view, this assertion is, of course, not at all a simple principle. It is fraught with difficulties of interpretation and definition. There is room for endless argument about how far it rested on a utilitarian commitment to the greatest happiness of the greatest number, as Mill said it did, and how far it rested, as Mill also said it did, on the belief that for the individual, 'in that part which merely concerns himself, his independence is, of right, absolute'. It is hard to see how these statements can both be right.

There is room for endless argument about how far Mill's defence of individuality rested on his belief in 'progress', and therefore on his semi-Platonic desire to encourage individuals of strong intellect and individuality – two things Mill too easily confused. If we take away Mill's belief that the best case will win in debate, large chunks of his argument suffer severe damage.

These are academic arguments, and they do not need to be resolved in a chapter which concentrates on Mill's political legacy. Few politicians have that philosophical an approach to their work, and to inject these questions into a political debate which hinges on the attempt to apply Mill's principle would be to lose one's audience. The political debates about the application of Mill's principle tend to hinge on two questions. One is the definition of the word 'harm', which is a much more complex question than Mill appreciated. The second, which tends to provide unconscious underpinning to most arguments about the first, is that there is still deep disagreement about whether, or how far, society stands in need of a common body of moral principles to allow it to work successfully. Opinion on this question has shifted very rapidly during my own lifetime, and it can be a shock to find, when reading the European Convention on Human Rights, to find how repeatedly it authorises government action 'for the protection of public morals'. That was drafted only forty-nine years ago, and one person involved in the preparatory work for it still sits in the House of Lords, where he still speaks in favour of the protection of public morals. It is hard to imagine such a phrase appearing in a present-day statute, though there are still many who would like to see it do so.

To Mill, the assumption that our moral principles were something we chose for ourselves was so deep as to be instinctive. He said: 'the only freedom which deserves the name, is that of pursuing our own good in our own way, so long as we do not attempt to deprive others of theirs, or impede their efforts to obtain it. Each is the proper guardian of his own health, whether bodily, or mental and spiritual. Mankind are greater gainers by suffering each other to live as seems good to themselves, than by compelling each to live as seems good to all the rest.' 'Human nature is not a machine to be built after a model, and set to to exactly the work prescribed for it, but a tree, which requires to grow and develop itself on all sides, according to the tendency of the inward forces which make it a living thing.'[6] This is now somewhere near the heart of what Liberals believe. The attempt to reduce all individuals to a bureaucratic formula, to be fitted in Procrustean style into the convenience of Whitehall statisticians, offends Liberals because it infringes precisely this principle.

Opponents of Mill's principle tend to undercut it by using the word 'harm' to apply to the spread of any conduct or opinion of which they themselves happen to disapprove. This, of course, begs every interesting question in the whole argument. I have no doubt that there are people in politics, many of whom I respect, and some of whom I would call my friends, who believe that the writing of this very chapter, in so far as it may be persuasive, is engaged in the act of doing harm. It is robbing society of that bond of common morality without which they believe it cannot safely function. In fact, as people engaged in counselling for social services departments know painfully well, there are not many pieces of advice we can give another human being which do not appear to someone to be harmful.

Mill meant something rather more precise than this. In his words, 'with regard to the merely contingent, or, as it may be called, constructive injury which a person causes to society, by conduct which neither violates any specific duty to the public, nor occasions perceptible hurt to any assignable individual except himself; the inconvenience is one society can afford to bear, for the sake of the greater good of human freedom'.[7] To be eligible for prohibition, harm must be certain, and it must be assignable.

Mill's criteria rule out any attempt to accuse people of doing harm simply by having a bad influence. In Mill's world, choosing which influences to succumb to is something responsible adults must do for themselves: they cannot rely on the state to do it for them. Moreover, except for the case of undue influence on a minor, a sick person, or someone otherwise unable to take full responsibility, it is impossible to show who has been harmed by a bad influence. It is simply suggested that someone somewhere *might* be harmed. Such harm is not assignable: there is no identifiable victim.

Perhaps the clearest example of how Mill handled the concept of harm is his famous corn-dealer passage: 'an opinion that corn-dealers are starvers of the poor, or that private property is robbery, ought to be unmolested when simply circulated through the press, but may justly incur punishment when delivered orally to an excited mob before the house of a corn-dealer.'[8] There can be few more lucid accounts of how to reconcile the imperatives of permitting free speech and prohibiting incitement to hatred. It must be admitted that when party members now discuss, for example, incitement to racial hatred, they do not always stick to this distinction. Mill does not enjoy biblical status. However, in any gathering discussing such questions, this view is one which will always be put.

Mill's is an optimist's world, in which reason tends to prevail, and one of the biggest justifications of liberty is the belief that in free debate the best case will prevail. It is not a world of demagogues and rabble-rousers. Not even Mill's admiration for Plato led him to fear the demagogic potential of democracy as Plato had done. Not only are there no demagogues: there is little of what the next generation of Victorians learnt to call 'the yellow press'. That optimism is characteristic of middle-class Victorian Liberalism, though slightly less so of popular radicals who brought a Calvinist conception of human nature with a history as Methodist lay preachers.

The assimilation of Mill's philosophy may have been put back a while by the sudden and terrible death of this Liberal optimism in August 1914. The shock of the discovery of the depth of man's inhumanity to man, of hatred, racial passion and cruelty, shows through in works like my father's *Autobiography* with a raw pain as if it had happened yesterday. He was not alone in turning away from Liberalism in response to that shock, and told me, as late as 1967, that he could never again vote for the party of Sir Edward Grey. Belief in the power of reason in human affairs was probably far lower in 1924 than it had been in 1914.

Yet the pessimism about human nature which 1914 engendered was only the creed which had been held by most of the party in the first century of its existence. Slowly, over the second half of the twentieth century, it has sunk in that a Millite commitment to liberty is perhaps even more necessary in a world where we assume, as indeed Mill himself did, that intolerance is one of the deepest and most abiding human emotions. The more we assume that, the more we need to put a very firm taboo on its outward and violent expression. The experience of Hitler affected many people, and by no means only Liberals, by making them more aware of the need to tolerate differences of race and creed, and to put a taboo on any violent expression of the dislike of difference.

Today, in the world of Drumcree, the murder of Stephen

Lawrence and the nail-bomb in the Admiral Duncan pub, it is much easier to say that enforcing at least an outward respect for diversity is part of the state's duties. It is part of its basic duty to keep the peace. It is among those who have grown up since Hitler that the views of Mill *On Liberty* have become, for the first time, part of the essence of the Liberal creed.

The creed has gained an extra boost from its obvious applicability to the sexual revolution of the 1960s. The contraceptive pill, which became regularly available in the autumn of 1962, changed sexual relations as fundamentally and as irrevocably as nuclear weapons changed the nature of war. The basis of all previous sexual morality had always been the fear of being left holding the baby. Now, though accidents still happen in the best-regulated families, people may reasonably hope that with care they can avoid that risk. This means that in sexual matters all the criteria of what is moral and what is not need to be rethought from the very beginning. That task is clearly one for the individual conscience, or rather for two individual consciences striving to reach agreement. Any answers which are to command confidence must be reached by people for themselves, and the intervention of government in the process, except in a few very limited contexts like the campaign of information on AIDS, is likely to be unhelpful. It is only if people's answers are their own that they will hold them with enough conviction to have any reasonable chance of acting on them. It is a world in which, whether we like it or loathe it, Mill's concept of individuality must inevitably hold sway. There will never again be a single agreed standard of sexual morals. Politics are far from having absorbed the shock-waves of this fact.

It is possible that the changes in sexual morals are far greater than any actual changes in sexual behaviour. My clearest abiding memory of the change of the sixties is of an elderly Oxford Fellow at High Table in 1969, complaining that undergraduates were no longer content simply to be able to have their girlfriends in all night: they were demanding a *right* to do so. It is that demand, rather than any change in behaviour, which encourages me to use the words 'sexual revolution'. The moral basis of authority has been changed.

One of the changes which came in during the sixties, which also drew on the declining social importance of religion, is the tendency for couples to live as settled partners rather than as married couples. This has cost politicians some effort of adjustment. Such changes, because they carry on by forces which are largely independent of politics, tend to hit politics accidentally and at oblique angles. This showed up in one of those sudden summer storms which hit the political process with Mediterranean suddenness. It concerned the Family Homes and Domestic Violence Bill, a minor Bill emanating from the Law Commission in the last years of the Major government. It passed through the House of Lords as an apparently uncontroversial Bill, and went down to the Commons, where it attracted the attention of the *Daily Mail*. The Bill allowed women who were victims of domestic violence at home to retain possession of the house, rather than having to escape to a refuge. The *Daily Mail* then discovered that this protection was extended, not only to wives, but to regular cohabiting partners. This produced a storm of protest from what is now known as the family wing of the Conservative Party.

The attitudes of the three parties to this Bill are instructive. The Bill was originally produced by a Conservative government, and was managed by the Lord Chancellor, Lord Mackay of Clashfern – hardly anyone's image of godless immorality. Nevertheless, the Conservatives felt unable to stand up against their family wing, even with the support of both the Opposition parties. Labour backed the Bill in its original form, but only a few of them with passion, and were prepared to let it go in the exchange of compromises at the end of the session. The Liberal Democrats, on the other hand, continued the fight to protect partners long after everyone else had abandoned it. There were liberals in all three parties, but only the Liberal Democrat party was made up of Liberals. This, no doubt, is what one should have expected, but it is unusually neatly illustrated.

The debate about whether marriage should be tax-neutral raises much the same issue about the status accorded by government to unmarried partners. This is an issue of which we are likely to hear much more in the remainder of this Parliament. It raises the question whether the decision to marry or live together as partners is a private matter, or whether the state has a legitimate interest in encouraging the ceremony of marriage. It is a classic Millite question, yet a few senior Liberal Democrats, clear philosophical Liberals, have nevertheless been influenced by a Christian heritage rather than by the sense that this is a private matter in which the state has no interest. The overwhelming majority of the party, on the other hand, can see no secular reasons why married and unmarried couples should be treated in different ways.

This debate is tending to broaden out into the question: 'What is a family?' To a Liberal pluralist, the tendency of Conservatives, and Tony Blair, to talk about 'the' family is offensive. The definite article is a monopolistic word, and tends to restrict. We may all agree that a married couple with children are a family. We may most of us agree that an unmarried couple living together with children are a family. After that, it gets a little more difficult. What of two orphan children being brought up by their aunt? Are they a family, and if not, why not? Are a stepfamily a family? If not, how many of us have been brought up outside a family for centuries? Is a widow with children a family? Again, usage has always taken them as such. If a widow with children is a family, why not a divorced or unmarried single parent with children? And what of a brother and sister, both widowed, who choose to spend their last years living together? And if all of these, why not two gay partners loving each other and living together?

Conservatives always ask at this point whether we are in favour of gay marriage. No doubt this is an important question for them, but in the light of the passages about partners above, I hope it is clear that it is not an important question for most of us. The important question for us is whether they should have the usual secular rights of partnership, such as survivor's tenancy and survivor's pension rights. Most of us can see no possible reason why not. By Mill's test, what possible harm can it do to anyone if they do?

We here come to some of the same problems in defining a family as have been discussed above in defining a nation. Neither families nor nations are God-given immutable entities. They have taken many different forms in different centuries and societies. Perhaps with families, as with nations, we need to adopt the subjective definition, that those groups are families who believe they are. That way, we let them decide for themselves whether they are a family or not. I once replied to a bishop who was arguing for the classic narrow definition of a heterosexual couple joined in Holy Matrimony that I preferred to adapt St Augustine's definition of a state: 'an assemblage of reasonable beings united together by a common agreement as to the objects of their love.' I am not certain whether this can pass for Liberalism, but I would like to think so.

We are, then, not only dealing with the famous headline issues like abortion and homosexuality, which are and are likely to remain free vote issues, even though they tend to leave us more united than any other party. We believe in conscience: we should respect it in others. We are dealing with something much larger than this. We believe that there is no one right way to live, and, provided they do no harm to others, people are normally best left to make such decisions for themselves. It is, after all, their lives we are dealing with, not ours, and they are much more likely to be able to decide how to live them than we are. We have never liked what Gladstone called 'grandmotherly legislation', or what is now called 'the nanny state'. We do not feel entitled to prohibit things just because we do not do them, or even because we dislike them. Our purpose in politics is not to get people to live in some single right way, but to help them to live in the way they think is right. It is the duty of the state to create opportunities, not to preach sermons.

This does not mean, as our opponents sometimes allege, that we believe 'anything goes'. The test of doing no harm to others can be a very stringent one, and we stick to it. Children must be cared for, whatever happens to their parents' love lives, and the responsibility of parents to maintain them must be enforced. Even though we do not like the present way of doing it, through the inflexible, illiberal and inhuman formula of the CSA, we insist the job must be done. Indeed, our objection to the CSA is in part that it is *less* effective in maintaining children than any alternative. This is because it insists on treating as like, cases which are only like in those respects that the formula happens to have foreseen, and are therefore wildly unlike when seen individually. Our commitment to returning such cases to the courts is part of our commitment to treating people as individuals. We defend this, among other reasons, because we think it will lead to children being more effectually supported than they are now. After all, it could hardly be much worse than the CSA.

The slogan of the Wolfenden Report, which led to the first steps to legalise homosexuality, was 'consenting adults in private'. This is a good Liberal slogan, and the vast majority of the party has adopted it as its own. In sexual matters, as in political ones, all power must rest on consent, and whatever has no consent is illegitimate. Rape is a crime, indecent assault is a crime, and sexual harassment is a crime. We put considerable effort into trying to improve the Bill against stalking, passed in the last Parliament. Where sex is a loving and willing activity, it causes us no problems. Where the demon of assault and violence peeps out behind it, it causes us very considerable problems. That is the point at which it begins to offend Liberal principles, and at this point we become, perhaps, more restrictionist than many others. It is not the alleged immorality which bothers us: it is the aggressive harm to others.

The word 'adult' was in the original Wolfenden formula again because of the importance of consent. The question what is an adult is again one on which there is room for some doubt around the edges. We are not fundamentalist about what constitutes an adult. What we insist on, on the usual free vote basis, is that whatever age may be chosen, it should be the same for both sexual orientations. That some people dislike an activity is no reason for imposing special restrictions. It is worth asking people who think otherwise to imagine a world with a homosexual majority, in which they tried to impose a higher age of consent for heterosexuals. That would clearly infringe the basic principle of equality before the law. Without that principle, there can be no political consent.

Real paedophilia, with children before the age of puberty, is a totally different matter. There is no way they can give a real consent, and where there is no consent, there can be no legitimacy. I cannot see Liberals ever changing their minds on this without abandoning their basic political philosophy.

The question of violence is much more difficult. In debates on censorship, 'sex'n'violence' are often lumped together as if they were a single issue, but in fact the two raise very different problems. Consensual sex with adequate contraception comes well within Mill's principle of doing no harm to others. Violence, unless it is between sado-masochists, does not. If depicting sex on television encourages people to sex, it does, within the usual limits, no harm to others. If it encourages violence, it does do harm to others. The question is one Liberals will have to think through quite hard.

There are many other places where Mill's principle of prohibiting what does harm to others has a restrictive, rather than a permissive, effect. Vandalism does harm to others: someone has to repair its effects, and someone has to pay for repairs to be done. Shoplifting does harm to others. Those who say the shop is too big to feel it are wrong. It adds approximately 1 per cent onto supermarket prices, and all the rest of us have to pay. Leaving litter does harm to others. I remember this being very forcibly explained to me by a pupil who had taken a vacation job road-sweeping for a council. After I had listened to his list of things he had to sweep up in the street, I felt almost as strongly as he did. Road rage or pushing in queues do harm to others. If anyone doubts it, let them consider how they feel if they are victims of these things. The classic test is always Locke's test under the principle of the law of nature: how would you feel if it were done to you? Where behaviour restricts the ability of others to live as they choose, Liberals may be in the forefront of moves to prohibit it.

We come into a much more difficult area when we come to the question of self-harm. Mill, in his 'one very simple principle', was adamant that 'his own good, either *physical* or moral, is not a sufficient warrant'. On the other hand, he also said that 'every one who receives the protection of society owes a return for the benefit'.[9] Is the relationship between these two principles changed by the advent of the Welfare State, in which physical self-harm imposes costs on our fellow-citizens? One might argue that this fact makes the action no longer self-regarding.

As a point of pure theory, this argument might well stand up. However, any breach in this wall must call for very great caution in practice. There is no risk-free activity. Even staying in bed is not risk-free, and our own kitchen or bathroom are among the most dangerous places where we can be. It would be absurd to propose a ban on using these rooms simply because they carry risk. While there are calls for the banning of boxing because of the risk of physical harm, there are none for the banning of football, swimming or mountaineering, all of which carry risks. One must therefore consider the likelihood that the feared risk will follow, as well as the degree of certainty that the feared effect is actually harmful. It is also necessary to remember Gladstone's strictures against 'grandmotherly legislation'. The ability to calculate risks is part of being safe out, and the inability to learn that skill may carry greater risks than anything.

It is also necessary to consider the question of enforceability. When some 30 per cent of the population do not consider an activity to be wrong, it becomes very nearly impossible to prohibit it. The number of dissentients constitute the proverbial blocking third. When this happens, prosecution becomes difficult because people do not give information, and because the police tend to give priority to something more universally unpopular. Even if there is a prosecution followed by conviction, punishment loses most of its effect if it is not shaming. The point when the person punished is seen as a victim is the point at which punishment ceases to deter.

It has become necessary to consider whether some or all of our present legislation against drugs has reached this point. I do not pretend to know the answers, and I offer none here. The party as a whole has done no more than call for a Royal Commission, to get the question thought through by people who do not depend on a political reputation. It is certainly true that present legislation and policy are getting nowhere. In general terms, even if it may be theoretically permissible to re-examine Mill's prohibition on measures inflicting self-harm, the task is so politically difficult that it could only rarely be undertaken.

Perhaps the biggest difficulty in Mill's principle, applied in a world which has tried to live by it for some time, is the subjectivity of the concept of 'harm'. As we move away from the concept of a common morality, it becomes steadily harder to know in advance what will be regarded as harmful by the person with whom we are dealing. What an American thinks is a welcoming smile may seem alarmingly aggressive in Japan. What one woman thinks is flirtation, another may think is sexual harassment. What one person thinks is cheerful rock music, his neighbour may think is intolerable noise nuisance.

The issue of noise pin-points the problem of deciding what is 'harm'. In common law, a noise becomes a nuisance if it is likely to annoy a 'reasonable man'. This standard is now very hard to apply. Does the 'reasonable man' own a stereo or carry a ghetto-blaster? The answer to this question will go a long way to determine what the law will regard as nuisance by noise. Yet any answer to this question, since it is culturally determined, will tend to infringe the principle of equality before the law.

Perhaps, as with the problem of defining a family, we are again driven back on the subjective. Harm to another person is what causes pain, and the only way of learning what causes pain to another person is to look and listen. When we know what causes them harm, we must try to avoid it, as they must try to stretch their tolerance a little in order not to infringe our liberty. The principle of live and let live, after all, is familiar anywhere where people live together, and to say a principle requires it is not to say anything so very dreadful.

In any case, the time of choice is past. We are never again going to have a common morality, whatever politicians may do. We have been to the moral Tower of Babel, and, especially with more movement around the world, the fact of different moral principles has become a fact of life. We must therefore learn to live with it. After Babel, the interpreter is king. We must observe the differences and respect them, because we have no other option.

How much common morality do we still need? The answer to this is that we need agreement only on one single thing. That is the need to keep the peace, which is the basic duty of society and of government. Anyone who attempts to breach the peace can be assumed to be likely to object if the same thing were done to him. That provides the one necessary ground for telling him it is wrong and restraining him. It is hard to imagine that there are many people who, as a matter of principle rather than of bloody-mindedness, do not want to keep the peace. With them, there can be no peace and no society, because they do not want it.

This is a problem for all political creeds. What Liberals can perhaps claim is that we are rather better adjusted to it than some others, because some of us have seen it coming.

Green Liberalism

Green Liberalism is so far the outermost layer of the onion of Liberal philosophy. It has only begun to grow within my adult memory, and is still growing rapidly. There is, of course, nothing distinctively or exclusively Liberal about the awareness that we face a threat to our environment. That rests on scientific evidence, of varying degrees of certainty, but of a bulk which is growing with alarming rapidity. That evidence is, of course, equally accessible to all parties, and while parties may like to claim to be more aware of it than others, this does not amount to distinctive philosophy. If the claim can be made out, it amounts only to superior alertness.

Where party philosophy shows up is in the reactions of parties who become aware of the risks. The Conservatives, when Chris Patten was at the Department of the Environment, became interested in the Pearce Report, which attempted to investigate mechanisms for setting a price tag on the environment. They reached instinctively for a market solution. Labour, now in office, turn instinctively to ways of discouraging car use by such devices as the notorious bus lane on the M4. They reach instinctively for top-down solutions. Liberal Democrats, while prepared to use both other methods in the right places, look instinctively for ways of controlling the exercise of power, both political and economic. Here we see the importance of a party philosophy. It tends to determine the areas in which parties look instinctively for solutions to new problems. Since governments of all complexions live hand to mouth, and rarely have time for real thinking, the choice of area in which to look instinctively is of great importance.

The realisation that we are capable of doing serious long-term damage to our own environment is a very new one. This is probably because it is only very recently that the human race has become sufficiently numerous, and sufficiently technically advanced, to have the power to do significant long-term damage. Our ancestors had frequent problems with occasional pollution. When the New River Company opened its supply of water to London, in the reign of James VI and I, there were complaints that people threw dead dogs and cats into the stream from which London's water was drawn. There is nothing new about this, and Green thinking, while it is always aware of such problems, tends to concentrate on the risk of more long-term, or even irreversible, damage.

I first learnt that human beings were capable of doing such damage in 1942, at the age of five, when I had a book containing photographs of the American Dust Bowl before and after over-intensive farming had led to soil erosion on a level which led to mass exodus and human disaster. I did not learn the right lessons. I thought this was a unique case, resulting from almost incredible criminal carelessness. I did learn that overgreedy pursuit of short-term returns could inhibit long-term prospects. On the other hand, because soil erosion is visible, and can be seen in a natural context, I thought it was only necessary to learn from observation to avoid repetition of any such disasters. I did not generalise from soil erosion in particular to risks of development in general. In this, I was probably typical of my generation.

We now know that many of the biggest environmental dangers, such as the loss of the ozone layer or global warming, are entirely invisible except to scientific instruments. In these cases, unlike that of the Dust Bowl, the link between cause and effect is not visible to the naked eye. We depend on science to establish it, and we have the worrying fear that by the time science is agreed, it may well be too late. We know, for example, that Mars once had an atmosphere, and now does not. We know, therefore, that atmospheres can be lost, but whether the damage to the ozone layer is subjecting us to a risk of total loss of our atmosphere is something we do not know, and have no dependable machinery for checking. We are travelling without a map.

We know from meteorological data that global warming has, to a significant extent, taken place in our own lifetimes. Yet we do not know whether this is a permanent or a cyclical trend. We know that within historic, and even more geological, times there have been massive variations in climate. We know that in geological times Britain in the age of the dinosaurs was semi-tropical, while in the last ice age Harrow on the Hill was the terminal moraine of a large glacier. In historic times, we know that in the little heat wave of the twelfth century, wine was grown on the south slope of Windsor Castle, while in the 'little ice age' of the seventeenth century there was perpetual snow on the Cairngorms. Are we witnessing another of these small cycles, or are we generating an irreversible trend? There is no way we can tell. We can only decide either to gamble on a risk, or to say 'better safe than sorry'. Greens must admit that many of the risks they depict are not certain. However, they are dealing in degrees of probability which appear increasingly high, and the risks of ignoring what they say are increasingly clearly unacceptable.

Global warming is largely blamed on greenhouse gases of which car exhausts are the most obvious source, while the loss of parts of the ozone layer is blamed on CFCs, which come largely from refrigerators. Yet banning the car or the refrigerator appear at present to be incompatible with democracy. Even more, they are incompatible with international order. One of the gravest problems of green politics is that of securing consent for what may be very urgent measures from countries which have not yet had the benefits of massive economic development. These countries naturally tend to say that benefiting from our own crime without letting anyone else join in is an unfair proceeding. The point has substance, and addressing it is extremely difficult. Once again, we face the problem of the lack of any international political order capable of addressing problems which cannot be tackled on a merely national level.

At the same time, we face the problem of a rapidly increasing world population. This is very largely a matter of scientific and medical advance. The increase in population in Sri Lanka, for example, is largely the result of the near-eradication of malaria after 1947. Such changes put great pressure on resources. It seems at present to be the majority view that we do not face an absolute shortage of food in the short term, but only a massive maldistribution. It is said that one could feed a substantial third world country on what goes every day into the dustbins of the United States. I do not know whether this claim is literally true, or who measured what is put into American dustbins. Yet the symbolic truth is real.

Inevitably, this increase in population increases the rate at which resources are consumed. Some resources, such as oil, are finite, and these will presumably be in due course exhausted, with consequences at which we can only guess. Others, such as fish, are renewable. Yet when the increase in consumption exceeds the rate of renewal, that increase becomes unsustainable. It cannot go on. I will not soon forget the time, back in the unregenerate days of 1979, when awareness of these issues was far less than it is now, when I rashly used the phrase, 'there are more fish in the sea than ever came out of it'. I found I was speaking to a Canadian Fishery Protection Officer, who spent the next hour explaining my error to me in words of one syllable. British fishermen now know all too well that the old proverb is not true. Yet the attempts by the European Union to control the rate of extraction, admittedly confused by the Major government's attempt to set up an open market in licences, have led only to outcries of 'national sovereignty!' One must again ask whether the necessary solutions are politically feasible.

Previous major resource crises have been met by scientific development. In 1906, we were on the edge of a transport crisis because our demand for horses was outstripping our capacity to grow oats to feed them. The problem was solved, without government intervention or understanding, by the invention of the internal combustion engine. A century later, we may wonder whether the cure was worse than the disease. Today, with the rapidly increasing power and volume of scientific research, the progress of new inventions is speeding up, and the modern risk is that they may be fed into use before we properly understand their effects. The use of organo-phosphate sheep dips, now confirmed to cause serious damage to the central nervous system, is today's example. We owe the exposure of this danger to one single Parliamentarian, the cross-bench hereditary peer the Countess of Mar. Having observed from a ringside seat the incredible effort it has taken her over the past nine years to penetrate the veil of official and commercial secrecy and obfuscation, I am not confident that future such dangers are easily avoided. I once described her as 'the only living evidence for the proposition that Parliament controls the executive'.

That memory does not fill me with confidence in watching the unfolding saga of genetically modified (GM) foods. Thinking about the world shortage of resources, and our still increasing population, I understand very well the desires which have led to research on GM foods. Even if there is not a gross absolute shortage of food in the world today, growing population must mean there soon will be. A Liberal commitment to cheap food which goes back to the Corn Laws is not to be cast aside at the moment when the world is likely to have most need of it. The impulse is sound.

Whether we can trust those in charge to deliver on it is a different question. Before doing something so potentially far-reaching, we need to know what we are doing. We need to know what the effects of the crops being developed are likely to be. That does not only mean the effect of eating them. It means the effect on bees, on cross-pollination and on diversity of species, among many other things. We should have known, long before we did, that the crops used in trials were cross-pollinating surrounding fields. We do not know what the effect of this on other crops is likely to be. Are we in danger of a sort of agricultural Gresham's Law? Gresham's Law says that bad money drives out good. Do bad seeds drive out good, and what will be the effect on the world's stock of crops? The story of organo-phosphates does not encourage me to believe that we will get truthful answers to these questions in the near future.

What then is distinctive in the assumptions Liberal culture brings to these problems? The first crucial decision, stated by Paddy Ashdown after the European Election of 1989, was that we would not turn our backs absolutely on economic growth. We would not join the fundamentalist wing of Green thinking. What we have done instead is to commit ourselves to the aim of *sustainable* growth. That is growth which does not so deplete resources or damage the environment that it prevents its own continuation. It is the opposite of Montesquieu's symbol of despotism: the tribe of

North American Indians who, when they wanted fruit, used to cut down the tree.

The key to the doctrine of sustainability is the concern for later generations: the object of power must be, not short-term gratification, but handing on something which can work for our children and our great-grandchildren. It is not something democracy easily encourages, yet democratic voters do have a concern for their children, and it is instructive to watch how often Paddy Ashdown in his speeches has called on it.

It also fits extremely well into traditional Liberal thinking about power which goes back to Locke. One of Locke's key ideas, borrowed unacknowledged from the Regicides who tried Charles I, was that power was a trust. There are three key points about a trust. First, the power is not the trustee's own: it is derivative, and comes from the trustor, in this case from the people who put the government there. The second is that trustees do not hold power for their own benefit. Power is a duty, and to be exercised strictly for the benefit of those who trust them. The third, and for our purposes the crucial one, is that the duty of the trustee is to hand on the inheritance to the next generation in as good a shape as he can leave it. In fact, sustainability is the trustee's essential duty. The failure to discharge this duty was once savagely illustrated in an *Observer* cartoon published at Christmas time sometime in the 1970s. The cartoon showed a large package, wrapped in Christmas paper and ribbons. On one side was written: 'Nuclear waste. DANGER. Do not open for 10,000 years.' On the other was written 'A present from Daddy'. That is the opposite of sustainability.

The doctrine of trusteeship involves a rejection of the pure free market concept of 'absolute property'. Property does not entitle its holder to do anything he likes with it to maximise its short-term profit. The owner has no more right to make it incapable of bearing crops than he has to burn it down for the insurance. It is a fraud on his posterity.

It has helped the party to absorb concepts of property so different from its cartoon image that so many of its most radical thoughts in the nineteenth century were about land. Land was a natural monopoly, and radical approaches to land, especially the doctrine of trusteeship, were designed to inhibit the exercise of monopoly power. A couple of quotations will illustrate the point, both from Primitive Methodists associated with the National Agricultural Workers' Union in the 1880s.

> God never intended the land to be in the hands of a few men who were no better than others. The land was made for the people, the people must live on it ... What was wanted was not nationalisation of land, but the unmonopolising of it ... They must instil into the minds of the landowners that the land was not absolutely theirs, but a trust held for the common good, and that in the use of it they are not to study simply their own pleasure and profit, but the public weal.

> The pervading principle of such tenure is, that landed possessions or holdings are a trust granted by the community or state, and the tenant or person holding it becomes a trustee or public functionary pledged to certain duties or responsibilities. And that this is the fundamental principle of land-tenure as set forth in the Bible will appear on examination.[1]

The Biblical verse cited, *Leviticus* 25.23, is where the Lord says that 'the land is mine'. It is typical of the mixture which has made this party that this Biblical fundamentalism is part of the chain of descent from John Locke to Paddy Ashdown. It is a side of Liberalism which the *laissez-faire* cartoonists would not recognise in a thousand years, and it makes the doctrine of sustainability secure and familiar.

On the issue of GM foods, we are sometimes accused by critics, including a few within our own party, of being anti-science. We are not, and have never been, any such thing, as Paddy Ashdown has gone to great pains to make clear.[2] Science we have always seen as an opener of doors and a creator of opportunities. What we want is time to bring the good science to bear on the issue. What we distrust is the power of money in politics. In that, we are heirs to a long history, going back to 1832 and beyond.

Anyone who followed the saga of organo-phosphates learnt the need to ask the sort of biographical questions Sir Lewis Namier used to ask about the interests of all the people on key committees, the sponsorship of research, and the funding of political parties. One of Margaret Thatcher's most regrettable legacies was the shift away from government funding towards commercial sponsorship of scientific research. As she should have foreseen, one of the results of this has been a diminished confidence in the research when it appears: it is subject to conflict of interest. It would be poetic justice if this were to lead people to disbelieve research which is in fact perfectly good, but it is the sort of poetic justice we should expect.

When we look at the unequal contest between a national state and an international company, we need to ask questions about commercial interests, not only in this country, but in the European Union, and in other countries such as the United States. It may be that what we are offered is perfectly all right, but, largely because of such questions, we do not yet know it. This distrust of money, the unelected power in politics, has been with us a long time, and we are not about to give it up. Until our politics is funded in ways less liable to create conflicts of interest, such problems are likely to recur.

We are also well aware that we are looking at an example of the modern problem of the imbalance of political and economic power. Because the sphere of operation of economic power is global while the sphere of operation of political power is merely national, economic power always enjoys the advantage of the fleet-footed boy over the flat-footed policeman: it is gone before action can be taken against it. It is not that economic power needs demonising: it is not always wrong. We do, though, need a healthy tension between it and political power, in which having the better case might have something to do with success. The state policeman should be able to give the economic boy a run for his money.

In the area of transport, we are again dealing with a need for political power. It is as obvious as anything can be that what is needed in environmental terms is a shift of traffic from private car to rail and other public transport. In many low-lying areas near the coasts, this may be essential to allow people, in the most literal sense, to keep their heads above water. It is not as if motoring in dense traffic were a great pleasure. Most of us only do it as often as we do because, in one way or another, the public transport on offer is not good enough to attract us. It may stop before we need to make our return journey. It may not go to the right place, or it may be too infrequent, too unreliable or too unsafe.

Nothing will be changed by exhorting motorists not to drive: that only annoys people without offering an alternative. It is the sort of task Napoleon left to Boxer, and Tony Blair leaves to John Prescott.

The only way to do anything is to spend money on providing an acceptable public alternative. When the carrots are in place, then the sticks can follow them, and if the carrots are good ones, the sticks will not need to be very big. Here it is relevant that, for all our desire to avoid waste in public spending, we have been a public service party ever since the construction of London's sewers in the 1840s. Public spending on doing what could not be done by individuals, or on creating choices people could not make for themselves, has always been a key part of the party's principles, and that is what is needed here. Our history gives us the ideological willingness to do it, and without that, spotting the need, as many others have done too, is nothing to the purpose.

In issues of international population, our unwillingness to impose moral codes saves us from the Scylla and Charybdis of Rome and Beijing, and enables us to follow a policy of creating opportunities for people to use contraception, while leaving the choice to them. There is nothing unique about that: we share it with many other British politicians of all parties, but at least the theoretical underpinnings for what is needed are very firmly in place. In these joint commitments, to firm Government action, and to preservation of individual choice, we would like to think we are the loyal heirs of a long history.

8

The Next Skin

So far, this book has described the growth of a series of skins of an onion which make up present-day Liberal philosophy. They cover a very wide range of themes and subjects, yet all of them revolve round the central heart of the onion – the need to control power. There is no reason to suppose this process has come to an end. Liberalism is not the sort of one-horse philosophy which has to talk of 'the end of history' when its horse drops dead. So long as human beings live on this planet (though that will not be for ever) the show will go on.

This chapter is an exercise in the highly dangerous art of gazing into a crystal ball, and trying to guess where another skin may be beginning to grow. It is necessarily doubly, even trebly, tentative. I am, to an extent, guessing where the major flashpoints caused by events are likely to be. That is a dangerous art: even where I can see a heap of barrels of gunpowder, they may not explode. If they do, the party may not develop new philosophy in response to them. If it does, it may not do it along lines I would expect.

It might be regarded as cheating to begin with an area where the party knows it faces a major conceptual challenge, and has already appointed a high-powered working group. That is the area of globalisation. This is a challenge to our thinking in three main areas, those of the economy, the environment, and foreign policy and collective security. In all these areas, we have mental furniture which will not fit in any of the rooms now available for it. We instinctively assume that politics is about the conduct of sovereign states, and that if we want to indulge in politics, the paradigm activity is that of forming policies we hope will be adopted by a

British Prime Minister and passed through a British House of Commons. Even I, even while I write these words, still instinctively think in this way. I am left over from the previous reign.

This is not because of any conscious political choices. It is not the result of the work of Euro-Federalists or conspirators against national sovereignty. It is the result of economic forces. Liberals are not economic determinists: we do not think we are helpless in the face of economic forces. We do think that the best way to control them is not to stand in front of the torrent shouting 'Stop!' It is, as Hercules found when he cleansed the Augean stable, to divert the torrent, and use its inherent force to do the work we want to be done. Before we can attempt this task, we must understand the force and direction of the flow of water, and identify its source.

Globalisation takes three forms: economic, environmental and military. Of these, the most important, and the source of the others, is probably economic. Recently, I was having lunch with a former pupil whose father is in the higher counsels of the Democratic Party in New York City. She told me he regularly had lunch with groups including politicians and bankers. In these, the politicians frequently began to talk on the assumption that they possessed economic power. The bankers had long ago given up trying to argue with them. They let them play with their toys until they were tired of them, and then got on with the job.

This was not because the bankers had an exceptional abstract devotion to the free market. It was because they knew the power of the politicians did not operate on the stage where economic power is exerted. The power of politicians operates within states, and real economic power now centres on the movement of money between states. This was the bankers' stage, not the politicians'. That is why, in present-day British politics, George Soros and his successors are more powerful men than Tony Blair. They control the accelerator and the brake: Blair only controls the heater and the window-opening buttons.

I do not propose to shoot the bankers: like Oscar Wilde's pianist, they are doing their best. On the other hand, any Liberal must dislike unaccountable power. A more even contest would be welcome.

Our present difficulties appear to have started with the collapse of the Bretton Woods agreement on the international currency market, in 1971. We should not blame this collapse on Keynes. The system, between 1945 and 1971, helped to give the world what may be the most sustained period of stable economic growth it has ever known, and that may be all one man can hope to achieve. It is worth remembering, also, that Bretton Woods as it came into operation was not the full scheme Keynes had conceived. In his scheme, there was to be an international reserve currency in terms of which the others were to be measured, and this was to be sustained by an IMF on a far grander, and more independent, scale than the one which was eventually created. As it was, this role of reserve currency which provided the measuring post for the others fell to the dollar, and it was this strain, in 1971, the dollar proved unable to sustain. Since 1971 the market, with increasing freedom, has moved currencies up and down as it saw fit.

People of my age have lived with the assumption that the major states were big players in the currency market, and that heavy intervention by the US treasury or the Bank of England was a big force in the market. This assumption is largely out of date. That is the result of the increasingly free movement of capital, encapsulated in this country in the Exchange Control Act of 1979. This means that everyone's savings (and we should remember before we get too moralistic that this includes all our pension funds) can move around the world at the drop of a hat looking for the best rate of return on savings.

Commentators are not agreed (and I do not have the independent knowledge to take my own line) how far this freedom of movement of money is the result of free market economic philosophy, which we could change, and how far it is the result of technological change, which we cannot. With the computer and the fax machine, the arrangements for electronic transfer of money within seconds have a sophistication of which people in 1971 could not even dream. Recent experience of the black market in the Russian rouble suggests that there is considerable technical difficulty in the way of any attempt to control this free movement of capital around the world.

That flow has reached a scale no government can easily think of controlling. Since 1973, international financial transactions have grown thirty times as fast as the growth in trade.[1] The volume of money which crossed British exchanges on Black Wednesday 1992 was almost equal to the whole of one year's GDP. As the government found on Black Wednesday, the contest between the state and a market of this size was a very unequal contest. It has been clear since Black Wednesday that our power to control the level of our currency is very limited indeed.

Sums of money of this size may be good for the host economies when they behave peaceably. When investors are alarmed, and money begins a stampede, the effects may be big enough to cause very serious disturbance. In July and August 1998, when the world believed it was looking into the abyss, four trillion dollars was wiped off the value of shares world-wide in only two months. In Britain alone, the stock market dropped some 300 billion dollars. The strain on banks of underwriting losses of this order is considerable.[2]

World economic competition is now necessarily very largely competition to provide host to these Odyssean savings travelling the world in search of a better return. That may be natural, but it may also become serious if the measures needed to attract savings are so detrimental to what, in old-fashioned language, we call 'the real economy' that it ceases to generate the money which gives rise to these savings. Keynes is no longer right that we can spend our way out of a recession. As Tim Congdon once pointed out with brutal simplicity, that can only be true so long as the rate of growth is higher than the rate of interest, and this is now hardly ever the case. On the other hand, Keynes remains right that the world economy cannot operate without a sufficient level of demand. If that disappears, a major slump will follow.

In this context, it must be serious that the free movement of capital is not, except inside the European Union, accompanied by any equivalent freedom of movement of labour. One need only watch the curl of the lip with which a minister in an asylum debate pronounces the words 'economic migrant' to realise that conventional wisdom has no thought of changing this. Capital may, and regularly does, move instantly to where labour is cheapest. Labour cannot move with equal rapidity to where capital is cheapest. This is not just a matter of the difficulty of uprooting people. It is sustained by a battery of controls on the freedom of movement of people, and there is every sign that states intend to make these controls more, and not less, stringent.

This is not a level playing field. Capital retains the power to force down the cost of labour. In many countries, especially those which still employ child labour, there is no floor under this power. Labour does not have enough power to force up its price to make it possible to claim that there is any sort of equal competition. Market theory is therefore irrelevant: the price of labour cannot find its own level, since it cannot move to it. Believers in pure free market theory ought to object to this as strongly as anyone else. It is a rigged market.

If the price of labour steadily falls, its purchasing power must fall with it. If its purchasing power falls, world demand must fall. If world demand falls, production must fall also. If production falls, there will be less capital available for investment, and at the end of the road, if nothing makes us reverse direction first, there must be a world slump. For twenty years, I told people writing essays on Marx that his prophecies of the collapse of capitalism were totally out of date, since Keynes had taught employers that if they set the level of wages too low, no one would buy their products. I do not tell them this any more.

These effects are exacerbated by the fact that governments need to pursue policies which attract, or at least do not repel, the investors who control the flow of this money *tsunami*. For example, they want high interest rates. If they do not get them, they tend to withdraw their money. Yet if they do get them, they cause no end of trouble to manufacturing industry, which not only finds its costs increased, but also finds, because of a rising value of the currency, that its export markets are diminished. The Euro, for example, is probably at present set at the right level for the real economy of Europe, and the low value of the currency will tend to encourage European exports.

Yet it is the wrong level for investors. They are not saints, and there is no reason why they should accept a rate of return 2 per cent lower than they could get in this country. Nor is there any reason why they should accept a return in a depreciating currency, for it will mean a great loss when they draw their pension. When money is invested in another country, the real return is a trade-off between three things, interest rate, inflation rate and exchange rate. I learnt this from personal experience when moving back to England in 1984 after five years working in the USA. Putting my American house on the market, I found its value had increased by 12 per cent in five years. Getting an up-to-date valuation of the English house I had sold five years earlier, I found its value had increased by 60 per cent. I then converted the change in the value of the English house into the dollars I would be bringing back to England, and found that, expressed in dollars, its value too had increased only by 12 per cent. That taught me the trade-off between inflation and exchange rate.

Yet to say no one is to blame makes the problem more serious. If we accept a need to take account of the interests of investors, that does not mean that it is healthy to allow them a total veto on economic policy. As soon as any economic force has that power, the market no longer operates. It is rigged just as if it were subjected to monopoly power. The interests of investors affect it in other ways too. They call for lower rates of taxation on saving, and set up a competition between host countries to make these lower than their neighbours. This creates a threat to the infrastructure of the host country. One Lord Mayor of London after another, protesting at the effect on the City of the underfunding of London Underground, has drawn attention to this problem, but no solution has followed.

If they are investing in manufacturing or services, they want low wages. Not merely do they want low wages, but they also want flexible labour markets. This means they need take no responsibility for labour in any off-season when they happen to want it. They offload their costs on the state, and burden the social security system of their host countries. It is the economic equivalent of tourists leaving litter.

Because more money is to be made out of money than out of work, the system produces gross inequalities. In Britain in 1996, the richest fifty people possessed more wealth than the poorest 5,5 million. In the world, according to the UN Human Development Report, the 225 richest people have wealth of more than one trillion dollars – more than the poorest 47 per cent of the world's population put together. This does not encourage a belief that money rewards effort. Also, in a world where 20 per cent of the population is responsible for 86 per cent of the consumption, it means the engine of economic growth is firing on one cylinder.[3] Apart from any concern for social justice, this degree of economic inequality is not economically efficient. Far too much energy is being wasted on the unpleasant task of policing the unemployed. Once again, principle and self-interest point in the same direction.

It should be easy for anyone who has followed this book this far to guess what I think should be Liberal reflexes to this situation. We face a totally unequal competition, which needs to be much better regulated to produce anything even vaguely resembling a level playing field. To this end, political power needs to be brought to bear on economic power.

That is easy to say, but it is not easy to do. We have seen since 1979 a massive shift in power from governments to markets. This has now gone so far that no single government can even think of reversing it. If it tries to do so unilaterally, it will merely put itself at an economic disadvantage against its competitors. François Mitterand, in 1982, learnt that Keynesianism in one country is an impossibility, and it has not been tried since.

If a large number of small players on the economic playing field find that, individually, they lack the power to compete against bigger forces, their obvious recourse is to form a cartel. This cannot be too obvious: for one thing, the competitive urge between nations will not disappear. Yet the range of competition may be narrowed. The other type of recourse is merger. The equivalent of this is to set out on the same route as international human rights law. To agree rules in international institutions such as the WTO or the ILO, and then incorporate these in domestic law is another possible route.

The nation states which face this money *tsunami* have both competitive interests and common interests. The common interests are to ensure that competition to attract savings does not lead them to inflict severe damage on their own domestic economies, to the detriment of the level of economic activity in the world as a whole. The Group of Eight, in pulling the world, for the time being, back from the abyss of 1998, showed this power to co-operate in a common interest. It does not demand anything more unthinkable than intelligence.

Commentators are at present attracted by the notion of restricting international foreign exchange transactions. This is the idea behind the Tobin Tax, which is supposed to reduce the volatility of international movement of money by putting a small tax on each transaction. I can see no theoretical objection to this: the problem is about its technical feasibility. If that is satisfied, we would still need to discover what its effects actually are. My own preference, at present, would be for competition more carefully regulated by international agreement and through international institutions. This would need to be done slowly and carefully: the law of unintended consequence applies as much in international as in domestic politics.

These are proposals for the internationalisation of political power. It is proposed that it be done, like the Pillars of the Maastricht Treaty, by co-operation between governments. This internationalisation of political power should create no problem for Liberal Democrats. Our leaders have been telling us for years that national sovereignty in economic matters is already dead. The choice is between international authority and international anarchy. Whether we have really taken this on board remains to be discovered, but at least the idea is not new to us.

The problem Liberal Democrats will probably fasten on is that which we have found with the European Commission, and even more with the European Council of Ministers. We do not like unaccountable power, and even more, we do not like secret power. Holding international power accountable to a vast variety of national institutions is a mug's game. Either it is totally ineffective, or it leads to the old Polish Diet problem of a situation in which everyone has a veto, and nothing happens.

We cannot propose holding back until we have cracked the problem of accountability. The situation is too urgent for that. Yet if we do not wait to crack the problem of accountability, we set ourselves a problem as thorny as the one we took on in the seventeenth century, when we began the task of holding a hereditary monarchy to account.

Mutatis mutandis, similar arguments apply to the globalisation of the politics of the environment, and of collective security. If we succeed in making real progress on these fronts, we will in the process produce a vast amount of thought about international political power. We must think about the source of its authority, its ends, its limits, its means of enforcement, and its account-ability. This will produce more skins to the onion that can even be imagined in this book.

EPILOGUE

A Distinctive Creed

This book has not been written as an exercise in inter-party polemic. It is intended as a positive statement of a creed, not as an attack on others. Yet one has not fully defined a creed unless one tackles the question of how it differs from others. The differences from Conservatism should be plain enough to readers of this book. The differing attitudes to national sovereignty, and to controlling the power of the market, run all through the book. The pluralism of our approach to morals is as clearly distinct from Conservatism as the pluralism of our approach to devolution.

If the task is trickier with Labour, it is because it is not yet certain exactly what New Labour believe. As a party, New Labour is barely five years old, and the defining events which force them to clarify their creed may be largely in the future. There is the further problem with Labour that they are at present a trinitarian formation of Old Labour, New Labour and Tony Blair. They may be three in one, but they are not always one in three. If we agree with one of these on a particular issue, it is not always the same one, and it remains an open question with which of the three we have most common ground. Tony Blair's professed sympathy with 'liberalism' is for a party of *laissez-faire*, which, as this book has attempted to show, has never actually existed. His attitude to us when he has learnt what we really stand for has yet to be discovered.

For some years, many Liberals attacking Labour have lazily confined themselves to a critique of 'Socialism', and have not always stated their own positive ideals, or, indeed, been reported when they did so. This book has been an attempt to take the welcome opportunity to restate the positive ideals. How do Labour differ from them?

The answers to that question vary from issue to issue, as well as from one Labour group to another. Within our own party, our attitudes to co-operation with Labour have tended to vary more according to the issues which most engage our interest than according to our intellectual genealogy. Those who see most unity of purpose have tended to be those whose priority issue was Europe. This makes sense. Ever since the sixties, Europe has been an issue which has produced alliances across parties, and that way of thinking is habit-forming. It is also, as a point of fact, very plainly true that with the Conservative Party travelling in its present direction, on that issue we have far more in common with Labour than with the Conservatives under present management. The question which remains open is whether this indicates a common attachment to the philosophy of pluralism, or whether it is a blip caused by a temporary departure from the centre ground by the Conservative Party. Only time will answer this question.

By contrast, the most hostile reactions to Tony Blair have come from those members of the party who concentrate on issues of poverty, inequality and oppression. Tony Blair's attachment to flexible labour markets and his complaints of 'welfare dependency' sound to specialists in these issues like a continuation of Conservatism by another name. Those with Labour conditioning (and this may include some ex-Labour members of the SDP) have persistently underestimated the intensity of Liberal hatred of poverty and of the inequalities of power it creates. On these issues, it is Old Labour and not New who provide us with our natural allies. The three biggest Labour revolts of this Parliament, on single-parent benefits, the Welfare Reform Bill and the Asylum Bill, have all united the Liberal Democrats with the Labour Left, and our natural allies have been Ken Livingstone, Jeremy Corbyn and Diane Abbott. Until we understand that this alliance is as natural as the alliance with Giles Radice on Europe, we will not understand what is going on.

It is these same issues which create the tension with Labour on public services. For Liberals since 1870, if not longer, public services have been an essential part of an assault on privilege. Without them, we cannot have a *carrière ouverte au talent*, in which people's prospects owe more to their ability than to the parental bank balance. Nor can we have the Rooseveltian freedom of freedom from fear unless we can know that our chances of recovery from illness do not depend on the level of our savings. Those Liberals who are driven by the egalitarianism which owes more to the *Magnificat* than to Marx used, as recently as 1992, to provide some of the keenest advocates of collaboration with Labour. Now, they provide its bitterest opponents. From this perspective, the change from Kinnock and Smith to Blair has opened up a new front of hostility. Blair as champion of the underdog lacks credibility.

By contrast, some of the most fruitful ground for collaboration has arisen from issues involving the Millite liberty of morals. For me, the moments of most whole-hearted collaboration with the government in this Parliament have been the two votes on the age of consent. I have had no complaint of the whole-heartedness of the government's commitment on this issue. It is probably the first government ever in which ministers could live with unmarried partners without giving rise to more than one neutral line of reporting in a newspaper. On these issues, it is Old Labour and not New who are the natural enemies. Many of them still belong to the old category of 'Comrade Blimp', and made speeches on the age of consent which were entirely indistinguishable from those made by the Conservatives. The fly in the ointment on this particular issue has been Tony Blair himself. He retains an attachment to 'the' family, with the definite article, which is very far from pluralist, and I was expressing anxiety about his attitude to single parents as early as 1994. John Redwood once memorably claimed that on that issue, Blair was to the right even of him. As an ally on moral issues, he must be handled with extreme care.

On Green issue, this government has achieved almost nothing, and they are in need of sustained and urgent criticism. They have two serious faults. One is the unwillingness to spend money, which means their transport policy lies in ruins. Occasional good intentions have provided the usual paving. The other, which shows up in their attitudes to GM foods, is the power-worshipping attitude to big business. This is part of a tendency, which recurs far too often, to kow-tow to the strong, and oppress the weak. A Prime

Minister who appeases Monsanto, but says, in his *Big Issue* article, that 'it is right to be intolerant of people homeless on the streets' has no claim to be a Liberal.

What of the very central issue, the heart of the onion, their willingness to control their own power? In the Human Rights Act, they have passed one measure which clearly passes this test, though it has yet to come into force. The Lord Chancellor, who was responsible for this Act, is, in spite of some appearances to the contrary, one of the ministers in this government with some claim to liberalism. It is only a pity that he was not equally successful with the other Bill which might have passed this test, Freedom of Information. In 1997, it appeared to many in the party that devolution might pass this test. So, in its long-term effects, it may. If it does, it will not be by Tony Blair's doing, since he has not understood that devolution in the state cannot work without devolution in the party. By attempting devolution without understanding this, he has opened a can of worms. Controlling his own power does not appear to be what he is in politics to do. If controlling the Prime Minister's power is his government's legacy, it will be by his failure, not by his success. There are some in his party, and even in its upper reaches, who do pass this test, but he is not among them. Thus, in the area of the very heart of Liberal philosophy, the need for opposition continues.

At present, though this is not a Liberal government, and on many issues we must oppose it accordingly, it is closer to us than the alternative, and it would be foolish not to recognise that fact. Yet this fact is not eternal. We are no closer to Labour now than we were to the Conservatives in 1955, which is perhaps the year of greatest closeness to them in my memory. The next year, we had Suez, and the closeness vanished in a puff of smoke. What will be in the next puff of smoke?

Notes

1. The Empty Hearse

1. Pat Thane, 'Women, Liberalism and Citizenship 1918-1930', in Eugenio F. Biagini, *Citizenship and Community* (hereafter Biagini, *Citizenship*), Cambridge (1996) p. 77.

2. G.R. Searle, *The Liberal Party: Triumph and Disintegration 1886-1929*, Basingstoke (1992) p. 173.

3. Eugenio F. Biagini, *Liberty, Retrenchment and Reform: Popular Liberalism in the Age of Gladstone* (hereafter Biagini, *Liberty*), Cambridge (1992) p. 161.

4. Biagini, *Liberty*, p. 2.

5. Reprinted in the *Independent*, 23 Jan. 1999.

6. Searle, *op. cit.*, p. 169.

7. Biagini, *Liberty*, p. 5.

8. Biagini, *Citizenship*, p. 211.

9. Searle, p. 73.

10. *Independent*, 23 Jan. 1999.

11. Searle, p. 110.

12. Biagini, *Liberty*, pp. 6, 16.

2. Controlling Executive Power

1. Jonathan Parry, *The Rise and Fall of Liberal Government in Victorian Britain*, New Haven (1993) p. 247. H.G.C. Matthew, *The Gladstone Diaries*, vols. xii-xiii, Oxford (1994) p. xlvi.

2. Private conversation. I am grateful to Tony Greaves for permission to reproduce it.

3. Biagini, *Liberty*, pp. 43, 50 and n.

4. J.P. Kenyon, *Revolution Principles*, Cambridge, 1977, p. 140.

5. Algernon Sidney, *Discourses Concerning Government*, ed. Thomas G. West, Indianapolis (1990) p. 21.

6. J.P. Kenyon, *op. cit.*, pp. 106-7.

7. Parry, p. 192.

8. Sidney, p. 113.

9. Private conversation. I would like to thank the Earl of Caithness, not only for a remarkably generous reaction to defeat, but for his permission to quote it.

10. Kenyon, p. 204.

11. Biagini, *Liberty*, p. 93.
12. John Locke, *Letter Concerning Toleration, Works* (1824) V 40.
13. Biagini, *Citizenship*, p. 14.

3. Pluralism

1. Biagini, *Liberty*, p. 161.
2. Kenyon, p. 86.
3. Biagini, *Liberty*, pp. 16-17.
4. Jo Grimond, *The Liberal Future* (1959) p. 38.
5. Biagini, *Citizenship*, p. 53. Vernon Bogdanor, *Devolution* (1999) p. 20.
6. Bogdanor, p. 117.
7. Biagini, *Citizenship*, p. 13.
8. *Ibid.*, p. 31.
9. Parry, pp. 116, 118, 64-5.
10. Parry, p. 241.
11. Biagini, *Liberty*, p. 103.
12. *Ibid.*, p. 320.
13. *Ibid.*, p. 12.
14. Kenyon, pp. 75-7.
15. Grimond, p. 15.
16. Biagini, *Liberty*, p. 80.
17. Martin Pugh, *Lloyd George* (1988) p. 78. My remark should not, of course, be taken to imply any sympathy with what Kitchener had done, but facing Lloyd George on the warpath on this subject is something I would not have wished on my worst enemy.
18. Biagini, *Liberty*, pp. 31-53, 105, 123, 151.
19. Reprinted in *Why I Am A Liberal Democrat*, ed. Duncan Brack, Dorchester (1996) p. 148.
20. Biagini, *Citizenship*, p. 51
21. *Ibid.*, p. 47.
22. Biagini, *Liberty*, pp. 159-61.

4. The Underdog and the Economy

1. Robert Skidelsky, *John Maynard Keynes*, Basingstoke (1992) II 219.
2. Karl Marx and Friedrich Engels, *Manifesto of the Communist Party*, ed. Engels, London (1888) p. 21.
3. Peter Mandler, *Aristocratic Government in the Age of Reform*, Oxford (1990) p. 241.
4. Michael Freeden, *The New Liberalism: An Ideology of Social Reform*, Oxford (1978) pp. 1, 33.
5. Searle, p. 26; Freeden, p. 35; Grimond, p. 22.
6. Biagini, *Citizenship*, p. 1.
7. Parry, p. 143.
8. *J.S. Mill On Liberty And Other Writings*, ed. Stefan Collini, Cambridge (1989) p. 95.
9. St Luke, 1.52-3, Biagini, *Liberty*, p. 99.
10. Biagini, *Liberty*, p. 98.
11. *Ibid.*, pp. 56-7.

12. Housing Consultation Session, Spring Conference 1999, 6 March 1999, Edinburgh. I am grateful to Ruth Coleman for permission to quote her.

13. Biagini, *Liberty*, p. 187.

14. Searle, p. 109.

15. Biagini, *Liberty*, p. 104 and n. Roy Jenkins, *Gladstone* (1995) p. 321.

16. Mandler, pp. 258, 241.

17. Searle, p. 66; Freeden, p. 45.

18. Parry, pp. 243-5; *Hansard*, vol. 252, 10 June 1880, cols. 1714-5.

19. Biagini, *Liberty*, p. 169.

20. *Ibid.*, p. 200.

21. Mill, p. 105.

22. Biagini, *Citizenship*, p. 42. Mill, p. 96.

5. Internationalism

1. Oral history. Communicated by my father to me on many occasions during my childhood, and by Lord John Russell to my father at Pembroke Lodge between 1876 and 1878.

2. Parry, pp. 189-90.

3. Jenkins, pp. 237-8.

4. Parry, p. 291.

5. Biagini, *Citizenship*, p. 12.

6. I am grateful to Eduardo Reyes for permission to quote him. At this distance of time, neither of us can remember his exact words, but he confirms that the thrust of his argument was as I remember it.

7. Paddy Ashdown, Speech at Chatham House, 6 March 1996.

6. Liberty to Do What, May I Ask?

1. Mill, pp. 69, 8.

2. Mill, pp. 8-9.

3. Locke, *Works* V 10-11.

4. Locke, p. 41.

5. Mill, p. 13.

6. Mill, pp. 16, 60.

7. Mill, p. 82.

8. Mill, p. 56.

9. Mill, p. 75.

7. Green Liberalism

1. Biagini, *Citizenship*, pp. 160-1.

2. Paddy Ashdown, Speech at South-West Regional Conference, Exeter, 20 Feb. 1999.

8. The Next Skin

1. *Guardian*, 14 Sept. 1998.

2. *Observer*, 6 Sept. 1998.

3. *Guardian*, 16 Dec. 1998 and 9 Sept. 1998.

Index